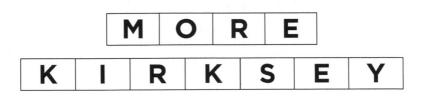

JUDGE BILL SWANN

BALBOA.PRESS

A DIVISION OF HAY HOUSE

Balboa Press books may be ordered through booksellers or by contacting:

Balboa Press
A Division of Hay House
1663 Liberty Drive
Bloomington, IN 47403
www.balboapress.com
844-682-1282

Because of the dynamic nature of the Internet, any web addresses or links contained in this book may have changed since publication and may no longer be valid. The views expressed in this work are solely those of the author and do not necessarily reflect the views of the publisher, and the publisher hereby disclaims any responsibility for them.

The author of this book does not dispense medical advice or prescribe the use of any technique as a form of treatment for physical, emotional, or medical problems without the advice of a physician, either directly or indirectly. The intent of the author is only to offer information of a general nature to help you in your quest for emotional and spiritual well-being. In the event you use any of the information in this book for yourself, which is your constitutional right, the author and the publisher assume no responsibility for your actions.

Any people depicted in stock imagery provided by Getty Images are models, and such images are being used for illustrative purposes only. Certain stock imagery © Getty Images.

Print information available on the last page.

ISBN: 978-1-9822-7589-1 (sc)
ISBN: 978-1-9822-7588-4 (hc)
ISBN: 978-1-9822-7587-7 (e)

Library of Congress Control Number: 2021921374

Balboa Press rev. date: 10/26/2021

CONTENTS

FOREWORD

Kirksey is back, but he may be a fool. His dealings with the dishwasher are a case in point.

As your author, I want you to know that I will speak in both the first and third persons. In those pieces in which the word "I" appears, obviously I'm speaking in the first person. In those pieces in which Kirksey speaks, he is speaking about himself in the third person: *"Kirksey did this. Kirksey thought such and such."*

This book ends with a section called "Thoughts." In the "Thoughts" section you will find some first person pieces and some third person pieces. In the "Kirksey" section, you will find only third person pieces with Kirksey speaking.

One other thing about the "Kirksey" section: Some of those pieces are speculative, looking at imagined scenarios. I have grouped those pieces together in a division of "Kirksey" called "What If?"

DEDICATION

Diana, as you know, in the Christmas carol the drummer boy gave his best skill to the Christ child.

My writing is the best that I have. I give it to you. I play my drum for you.

KIRKSEY: WHAT IF?

KIRKSEY WONDERED ABOUT DARKNESS

Was it sentient? Did it have emotions? If so, perhaps it got bored being shut up in the closet. It might want to get out. That would be reasonable.

How could it get out? Maybe it could become a liquid. If it could do that, it would not have to open the closet door. The darkness could simply flow out under the closet door. It could flow out under the door and across the floor.

If all the darkness flowed out of the closet, what would be left behind? A vacuum? No, not possible. Air would be sucked in under the closet door. There wouldn't be a vacuum.

But, if all the darkness flowed out, would it be light inside the closet? Maybe. Kirksey did not know. He was sure, however, that it was dark inside electric refrigerators when you shut the door. Reasonably sure.

KIRKSEY WONDERED ABOUT EATING BOOKS

The Tooth Fairy had given him three books to eat. Not to bite, chew, and swallow, but just to place against his head so that all the content would go into his understanding. Everything that had been inside the books would then be inside him.

Kirksey wondered what he would choose. Kirksey thought probably one of them should be a foreign language textbook, a big one so that he would really master the language. But then he thought, okay, which language? And then he wondered if he really wanted to expand to new languages. He was already fluent in German, and his Spanish was pretty good. Wouldn't it be better to build out one of those two languages? He didn't know.

He also thought about the Oxford English Dictionary. He could hold it against his head and know everything that was in there. But did he really want to know that much about the history of the English language? He certainly didn't need the OED for vocabulary. Kirksey's vocabulary was already super.

What about the Bible? That might be an excellent choice, because Kirksey had a lot to learn there. How about the latest volume of *The Joy of Cooking*? Kirksey was a pretty good cook but he only did a few dishes. That sounded pretty good. What about an up-to-date atlas of the world? Countries were changing their names all the time now, and Kirksey was way behind. What about the complete works of Shakespeare?

So, he had two of the three at any rate: *The Joy of Cooking* and the Bible. But what about that language? Wouldn't it be cool to pick up Mandarin or Arabic? And what about that atlas of the world? What about the works of Shakespeare? He would have to think about it. Maybe he could go back to the Tooth Fairy and ask for six books.

KIRKSEY WONDERED ABOUT THE FOOTBALL ITSELF

Kirksey had been thinking about the game of football. What if the ball were different? What would happen?

Say, change it to a soccer ball.

The kicking game would improve. The passing game would not. Passing would still be possible, but catching a soccer ball on short quick passes would be harder than catching a normal football. Long passes would be easier to break up than passes done with a normal football. With runs, the ball could be held with one hand, but for security it would have to be held with two hands. That would slow the run game down. The game might simply become a kicking game, with field goals galore.

Or, change it to a tennis ball. What would happen? Unless the kicker's footwear were changed to something akin to a tennis racket, the kicking game would be strange: punts would be erratic, next to impossible, and kickoffs would be shorter, leading to fewer touchbacks. The passing game would improve because the ball would be easy to throw accurately. There would be virtually no fumbles, so the run game would improve.

But say the ball became a ping pong ball. What would happen? Assuming the kicker could equip his shoe with a ping-pong paddle, it would be possible to do kickoffs longer than ten yards, so all would be well there. Field goals would degrade hugely. The passing game would be difficult, next to impossible. There would be no fumbles, so the run game would be the go-to option.

Say the ball became a golf ball. What would happen? Assuming that the kickers could wear fancy footwear, making each shoe correspond to the desired golf iron, the kicking game would blossom. Touchbacks on kickoffs, if that's what was wanted. Or high hang times, for tackles to be made close to the goal line. The passing game would probably degrade, due to drops and interceptions. The run game would be massive because there would be no fumbles.

KIRKSEY THOUGHT ABOUT THE SUN

Kirksey was a prayerful man. He was grateful for his life. He thanked God every day for one more day of life. And yet he came up with a scary thought. One day he watched the sun rise to the left of Mount LeConte and he asked himself what if it didn't happen? What if the sun did not come up?

He knew that, ultimately, it meant death for all the world, for all living things except those at the bottom of the ocean which already lived without light. He wondered, would those creatures eventually evolve to come up to the top, after eons crawl up on the land, and live there in the bitter cold darkness? Kirksey didn't know. He didn't want to think about it.

KIRKSEY SAW "BIBLES 20% OFF"

It was a sign in the window of a Christian bookstore. He wondered if those bibles had all the words. If not, which 20% had been cut? What part of the bible did someone think was expendable?

Certainly not the creation stories, even though they could do with some reconciling. Certainly not the four gospels, nor Acts, nor the Pauline letters. So, maybe it was some of the arcane stuff in the Old Testament. Maybe that was the place.

Kirksey wondered whether there had been a commission to make the decisions, as there had been when the King James version came into being. He hoped so.

KIRKSEY FOUND BRAIDED LINE ON HIS FATHER'S OLD REEL

Kirksey had found braided line on his father's reel. His dad had put it on the reel in the 1950's, back when he had fished in Panama City, Florida. And now the technology was back. The latest and greatest fishing invention, "Spider Wire" and its competitors.

It is great. It gives you intimate contact with the bottom, if that is how you are fishing, say bumping a crawdad lure along the bottom. And if you get hung up, you can just pull loose without fear of breaking the line.

Kirksey wondered whether other things would come back–manual typewriters, onion skins and carbon paper, office windows open in the summer, desk fans rotating, legal secretaries clacking away in the summer heat.

KIRKSEY

KIRKSEY'S MOTHER GOT A SUN LAMP FOR CHRISTMAS

Kirksey had the job of putting up the Christmas tree each year. His brothers were not old enough to help. The family did not have a tree stand, so Kirksey would make one out of a bucket of wet sand. But first he would cut a half inch off the stump of the tree so that it could drink water from the sand. And he would add water to the sand from time to time.

The lights went on first. Hot pointy ones, the kind where when one burns out, the whole string goes dark. Then the decorations went on, including the star on top. Some Christmases Kirksey would spray snow from an aerosol can on the branches. Last of all the tinsel, in individual strands laid on.

Kirksey was maybe fourteen or fifteen years old. It doesn't really matter when it was. The sun lamp happened. Kirksey's father gave his wife a sun lamp. It was all wrapped up, a big thing, four and a half feet tall. Kirksey's mother got the paper off. There was a black hood on top and a black heavy base on the floor. Kirksey's mother was delighted. "Oh, a hair dryer!" she said.

"No, damnit," said Kirksey's father. "It's a sun lamp."

"Well," said his mother, "You can use it for a hair dryer."

His father said, "Shit. Open something else."

KIRKSEY'S FATHER TAUGHT HIM TO SHOOT

Not every sort of gun, but shotguns definitely. This was at the Knoxville Rod and Gun Club: 16-yard trap and handicap. Kirksey also took turns as a loader in the trap houses, placing clay targets on the powerful, dangerous arm which flung one (or in doubles, two) targets on the command of the scorer.

When Kirksey was in junior high school, 1954 to 1956, his father took him to the Athletic House. Kirksey's father thought it was time Kirksey had a rifle.

Kirksey had just come back from Boy Scout Camp Pellissippi in Anderson County. He had won the camp's marksmanship award. It turned out Kirksey was a natural with a rifle. More on that award in a moment.

The rifle he had used at camp was a single-shot .22. The camp had ten of them. Firing was from the prone position. After a few days Kirksey put a group of five through one hole. True, the hole was slightly larger than what just one .22 slug cuts out, but not by much. His instructor, who was Persian, was astounded. He said that the very slight enlargement of the hole was "probably due to the rotation of the Earth."

That sounded pretty good to Kirksey at the time, good enough that he believed it.

The award from the instructor was a pin-on Iranian flag. Kirksey put it on his uniform right away, being careful not to stick himself. Kirksey still has it today, along with his merit badge sash. The Persian instructor could not make the English "th" sound, pronouncing it "t." All the campers loved hearing him say "my turd week at Camp Pellissippi."

The vagaries of history, of course, make Kirksey's teacher's award, his kindness, and his instruction particularly precious today.

Anyway, Kirksey's father was impressed enough that he put more guns into his hands. He bought Kirksey a thirty-two inch full choke single-shot Ithaca 12-gauge. That's the gun which had set the world's record for consecutive broken targets.

Kirksey has two shotguns now, five rifles, and four handguns, but his favorite gun of all is his Marlin lever-action .22, the one his father bought him at the Athletic House. Kirksey didn't know then that it was Annie Oakley's gun. Of all his guns, this is the one Kirksey will give to his child or grandchild who turns out to be the best shot.

Kirksey's dad did not introduce him to handguns, the third form of firearms. Kirksey took that up on his own and introduced his brother to it. That brother quickly surpassed Kirksey in handgunning but that brother never developed much skill in shotgunning. Kirksey also introduced his brother to spin fishing, and the brother before long surpassed him there as well.

Of course, Kirksey was competent with a BB gun, the fourth form of firearms, and his brother was an extraordinary shot with a pellet gun, the fifth form of firearms.

KIRKSEY'S FATHER
AND CAMP KILMER

Located in Central New Jersey, Camp Kilmer was a former United States Army camp that was activated in June 1942 as a staging area and part of an installation of the New York Port of Embarkation. The camp was organized as part of the Army Service Forces Transportation Corps. Troops were quartered at Camp Kilmer in preparation for transport to the European theater of operations in World War II. Eventually, it became the largest processing center for troops heading overseas and returning from World War II, processing over 2.5 million soldiers.

It officially closed in 2009. The camp was named for Joyce Kilmer, a poet killed in World War I while serving with 69th Infantry Regiment. He wrote "Trees":

> *I think that I shall never see*
> *A poem lovely as a tree.*
> *A tree whose hungry mouth is prest*
> *Against the earth's sweet flowing breast;*
> *A tree that looks at God all day,*
> *And lifts her leafy arms to pray;*
> *A tree that may in Summer wear*

A nest of robins in her hair;
Upon whose bosom snow has lain;
Who intimately lives with rain.
Poems are made by fools like me,
But only God can make a tree.

When Kirksey's father was temporarily on the west coast, he wanted to let his wife know that he would soon be on the east coast at Camp Kilmer, where they might see each other. But he was forbidden by the Army to tell her that. So he sent her a telegram with one word, *"Trees."* It didn't work. Kirksey's mother didn't figure it out.

KIRKSEY AND USING THINGS UP

Kirksey was cheap. It was because he was Scotch-Irish. He would not waste. He would not discard a jar or a squeeze bottle with any contents he had paid for.

There was a tangible joy in finishing something. He knew this was essentially silly. But that was who he was.

It was the same thing with repairing an object. He would repair and repair rather than replace the thing. It was the satisfaction of getting more use from something. Scotch-Irish.

KIRKSEY'S GRANDDAUGHTER AND THE OCTOPUS

When Marren learned that the octopus has three hearts, she said, "He must be able to love so much more than we can." Kirksey melted at her unsullied naivete.

The reason for the octopuses' impressive cardiac system is probably the unusual composition of their blood. Unlike vertebrates, which have iron-rich hemoglobin packed into red blood cells, octopuses have copper-rich hemocyanin dissolved directly in their blood. This means their blood is blue.

Hemocyanin is less efficient than hemoglobin as an oxygen transporter. The three hearts compensate for this by pumping blood at higher pressure around the body to supply the octopuses' active lifestyle.

KIRKSEY DIDN'T KNOW WHERE HIS RIGHT FOOT WAS

Most of the time. He had to look down to know. The Stryker corporation had done that to him. Oh, they hadn't meant to. It was just that they had produced a metal-on-metal femur and ball socket, and his doc, an excellent surgeon at the Knoxville Orthopedic Clinic, had used it. After two and a half years, Kirksey had cobaltism (metal poisoning), a failed right hip replacement, abductor avulsion, and a pseudotumor.

Kirksey talked to his doc about what to do. He was willing to do the "revision" of Kirksey's hip, but he did not want to. He said revisions were difficult, and should be done by someone who did a lot of them. So Kirksey went to the Mayo Clinic in Rochester, Minnesota, to a surgeon who did six or more revisions every week. That doctor found all of the above, grey rotted muscle, and a smelly mess. He put in a Johnson & Johnson hip.

Stryker then paid Kirksey a little money as part of a class action lawsuit. There were a lot of bad Stryker hips out there. But Kirksey wanted his leg back.

KIRKSEY AND THE DISHWASHER

Kirksey didn't think he was a fool, yet what happened with him and the Gatlinburg dishwasher made him wonder.

He had run out of dishwasher pods. So he went halfway down the hill to a small market and picked some up. There was no choice, just one kind, made by Tide.

He put a pod in the dishwasher and turned it on. Pretty soon there was foam coming out under the door hinge on the front of the dishwasher. So much foam came out that it soaked the rug in front of the dishwasher. Kirksey figured he had improperly put a large mixing bowl in the dishwasher. So he rearranged the mixing bowl and started over.

It was no better. More foam came out. Kirksey kept sopping up the foam with paper towels until the wash cycle ended. The dishes were clean so he took them out and stored them away.

The next day Kirksey had another load of dishes to wash so he put in a pod and experienced the exact same thing again. At this point he decided he should call Diana.

She immediately told him that Tide pods were for washing clothes, not dishes. She said he should run the dishwasher many times with no dishes until he had rinsed all the Tide from the dishwasher system. Kirksey did this. Then he bought real dishwasher pods from Food City and all was well.

Kirksey found it interesting that he had come up with an intelligent, alternative, and completely incorrect explanation for the misbehavior of the dishwasher; it had had nothing to do with the placement of the mixing bowl.

Diana told him later that grocery stores made sure laundry products were in one aisle and dishwashing products in a completely different aisle. Kirksey thought this seemed to indicate that other men had made the same mistake. Perhaps even women.

KIRKSEY HAD BEEN DISHONEST AS A CHILD

He had been stealing from the family grocery money, when he lived in Hyde Park outside Boston. Well, maybe it wasn't exactly stealing. If he had been old enough, he might have considered it creative diversion of the grocery money his mother had given him.

His mother would send him to the store, a tiny grocery three blocks away. The purchases were always small--a loaf of bread, three onions, meat of some kind. Milk was delivered to the door by the milkman, so Kirksey never had to buy milk.

Kirksey would get home with the purchases, give his mother the change, and all would be well. But one day his mother said, "That man is cheating you again. We'll just go see about this." He and his mother went to the store. She was carrying the bag with the purchases.

The grocer said, "Yes, three onions, the liverwurst, Merita bread, and six pieces of candy." "Oh," said Kirksey's mother, looking at him. They went home.

When Kirksey's father got home, his mother told him what Kirksey had done. And had been doing for a while. His father told him to get his piggy bank. It was made of yellow glass, and had a slot on top, where you could get the pennies out, but you could only do it by putting a table knife inside to line up the pennies so they would fall out. Kirksey's father made him take all his pennies out and give them to him. Kirksey's mother was crying. Kirksey was crying. No more dishonesty. Ever.

KIRKSEY AND THREE COLORS OF BEAR TAGS

In the Great Smoky Mountains National Park, euthanasia is always the last option for bears. The first effort is to capture the bear and release it elsewhere within the park. That leads to a green tag. From then on it is green to yellow to red, a three-strike system.

The second time he is encountered, he gets a yellow tag. The third time he gets a red tag. When and if he is encountered wearing a red tag, his game is over. He can't be relocated. That just exports the problem. So it is time for him to go to heaven.

Regardless of whether he is on the tag system or not, every bear found scavenging on human remains is killed.

KIRKSEY HATED YELLOW JACKETS

Two had gotten him yesterday. Or maybe it was only one that had stung him twice. He couldn't tell. Yellow jackets don't die when they sting. They inject venom and then withdraw, to fly away, to sting you again another day.

The honeybee can only sting once. Her stinger attaches to you and pulls out a good portion of her abdomen. So she dies. It is a suicide mission.

Kirksey couldn't see God's plan here. Honeybees were valuable. As far as Kirksey could see, yellow jackets were worthless.

KIRKSEY KNEW THAT HE DRESSED FOR OTHERS

He did it because it met their expectations. He wanted to give them what they were anticipating. He knew that if he did less than dress properly it would confuse the others. They could think, *"Well, here's Kirksey, and he looks like a slob. He doesn't care what impression he makes."*

Kirksey felt it was not an exaggeration to say that it honored people to dress for them. If he did less than what was expected of him there would be an effect, and not a good one.

Then there was that whole thing about hats inside the house, inside a restaurant, even--horrors!--baseball caps. Of course, Kirksey knew there was no logical reason not to wear anything you wanted on your head whenever and wherever you went. But there it was. You just didn't do it.

KIRKSEY KNEW GOD MADE THE CLOUDS

The question was, why didn't he pay more attention to them? Maybe because he had them all the time? So he took them for granted? He did not take roses for granted. Was that because he did not have roses all the time? Was that it?

Then he thought, we take some people for granted because they are always around. "Yes, they're wonderful people. Yes, we love them." But we treat them as part of the landscape.

Perhaps, he thought, clouds can be a lesson to behave better to the people around us.

KIRKSEY OWNED 50 ACRES IN SOUTH KNOX COUNTY

He had owned it for decades. It was a square south-facing ridge with eight acres of flat land at the bottom with grass. One of the neighbors asked whether he might grow hay there for himself and Kirksey had been delighted. The neighbor cut hay for several years and then moved away.

The eight acres grew up with bushes and small trees and then larger trees. The hilly forty-two acres extended all the way to the ridgetop and over the back. The highest point had a view of Mount LeConte. Kirksey at one time had considered building a house, but it was so remote Diana did not like the idea. So the land went unattended.

Kirksey learned his land had turned into a dump for household trash. That made no sense because there was a free, tax-supported Knox County dump center two miles away. But some people thought it was preferable to offload garbage onto Kirksey's land—old tires, broken plastic toys, plastic sheets, beer bottles, bags of household garbage, garden hoses.

Kirksey learned of this when a crew from Knox County went out and cleaned up one pile near the road, sent him a bill for it, and placed a lien on the fifty acres to assure payment of the cleanup cost. That got Kirksey's attention.

Kirksey went out with a friend and worked all day cleaning up more of the trash. Then he fenced the land and put up *no trespassing* signs.

A good thing which came out of the experience was that he met new neighbors, delightful people. They had a sign on their picket fence reading, *"Gardener wanted. Must look good bending over."*

He also met Ray Sexton as he was planting potatoes. Kirksey and Ray talked about gardening that day, and many days thereafter. As the summer went on, Ray shared his zucchini, his yellow squash, his cucumbers.

KIRKSEY USED HIS OWN STAMPS

When Kirksey had been a judge, he always kept his own supply of stamps for his personal mail. He simply would not put his personal correspondence, bills he was paying, thank you notes, into the judgeship's outgoing mail. That would be wrong, and Kirksey felt strongly about that.

However, when he retired in 2014, he took with him a souvenir, an old creaky wooden chair. He had put his briefcase onto it every day for thirty-two years. It was his friend. Kirksey thought the chair's previous life had involved seating alternate jurors. That was not important. The important thing was that Kirksey was taking a piece of state equipment. Or maybe it was county equipment. It didn't matter which, it belonged to the public, and Kirksey was taking it.

He could have written a check to the county or to the state to pay for the chair, but he felt that to do so was excessive, even talmudic.

KIRKSEY BELIEVED CERTAIN POEMS COULD NOT BE FORGOTTEN

At least parts of them. That is, once you heard them, they just stuck with you. Whether because of meter, image, or the simple flow of sound, there it was.

Poe's "Raven":
Once upon a midnight dreary, while I pondered, weak and weary,
Over many a quaint and curious volume of forgotten lore—
While I nodded, nearly napping, suddenly there came a tapping,
As of some one gently rapping, rapping at my chamber door.
"'Tis some visitor," I muttered, "tapping at my chamber door—
Only this and nothing more."

Tennyson's "Tithonus":
The woods decay, the woods decay and fall,
The vapours weep their burthen to the ground,

45

Man comes and tills the field and lies beneath,
And after many a summer dies the swan.

Sidney Lanier's *"Marshes of Glynn"*:
Glooms of the live-oaks, beautiful-braided and woven
With intricate shades of the vines that myriad-cloven
Clamber the forks of the multiform boughs . . .

Hawthorne's *"Evangeline"*:
This is the forest primeval. The murmuring pines and the hemlocks,
Bearded with moss, and in garments green, indistinct in the twilight,
Stand like Druids of eld, with voices sad and prophetic,
Stand like harpers hoar, with beards that rest on their bosoms.

Heine's *"Lorelei"*:
Ich weiss nicht, was soll es bedeuten,
Dass ich so traurig bin;
Ein Märchen aus alten Zeiten,
Das kommt mir nicht aus dem Sinn.

I don't know what it means
That I am so sad
A legend of bygone days
That I cannot keep out of my mind.

KIRKSEY AND THE PC

Kirksey knew he was definitely a creature of habit. Under his usual habit of working, he had always commenced work on his desktop PC--whether at home or in Gatlinburg--by clicking the icon which opened all of the things he needed.

Then one day he needed to transfer photographs from old floppy discs to the PC. Kirksey thought this was no big deal. He bought a Tendak unit to do it. He thought he could march forward with no problems but he was wrong. It just wouldn't work. He ended up chasing his tail for an hour and realized it was time to call Karl Ricker. After all, Kirksey thought, it was Karl who had told him to buy the Tendak unit.

Karl taught him that he had to be off the internet to do what he was trying to do. Until that moment Kirksey had never grasped that there was a world of difference between being open to the internet, and getting some small tasks done in a compartmentalized world off of the internet.

KIRKSEY'S GRANDMOTHER HAD BLUE WILLOW CHINA

And Kirksey had always loved it. But Effie had died years ago, and now when Kirksey thought back, he realized that Effie's blue willow had meant tea time, and that tea time had meant neighbors would drop in. Kirksey saw now that this was an extended community usually absent nowadays.

So what? His love for the Blue Willow was there just the same. Kirksey had bought some in honor of Effie. He had it in his big house in Gatlinburg. Some of his blue willow in Gatlinburg was old: Kirksey had inherited that from his mother, Effie's daughter Jeanette. But the best of Kirksey's blue willow was new, Johnson Brothers china, bought on the internet.

Kirksey had learned about blue willow's long manufacturing history. He had also learned that the pattern told an involved and not very happy story:

Long ago, in the days when China was ruled by emperors, a Chinese mandarin, Tso Ling, lived in a magnificent pagoda under branches of an apple tree. There was a bridge down the hill from his pagoda. A wispy willow tree drooped over the bridge. Tso Ling was the father of a beautiful girl, Kwang-se. He had promised her as a bride to an old and wealthy merchant. She, however, fell in love with Chang, her father's clerk. She and Chang eloped across the sea to a cottage on an island. Tso Ling pursued and caught them. He was about to have them killed when the gods transformed them into a pair of turtle doves. The birds now fly high in the sky next to Tso Ling's apple tree.

Even though blue willow has a Chinese look and story, it was actually created in England in 1780 by engraver Thomas Minton. Minton then sold the design to potter Thomas Turner who mass-produced the pattern on earthenware. This became known as chinoiserie, European interpretations of Chinese decorative styles.

Blue willow began as transferware. Designs were transferred rather than hand-painted. Eventually blue willow became prime working-class dinnerware, made by 500 different makers.

The "Blue Plate Special" started at diners in the 1920's. It typically featured a big meal for a low price, served up on a blue plate. Many believe that the preferred dish was the blue willow "grill plate" which had separated areas for an entree and sides.

Johnson Brothers blue willow is now available in a twenty-piece set for $134.99 from Bed Bath & Beyond. It is simply gorgeous.

KIRKSEY WENT TO FORT DICKERSON: THE CIVIL WAR DEFENSE OF KNOXVILLE

In simplest terms the battle for Knoxville pitted General Burnside for the Union against General Longstreet for the Confederates. Burnside won.

The Confederacy sent an army into East Tennessee. Under the command of General Longstreet, Confederate forces made a concerted effort to recover the region and destroy Burnside's army, November and December 1863.

Knoxville was a pro-Confederate town of some 3700 persons when Tennessee seceded from the Union in June of 1861. It was the commercial and light manufacturing center of East Tennessee, and a region of considerable agricultural importance. It provided large quantities of wheat, corn, pork and other foodstuffs to areas beyond the great valley of the Tennessee River.

Knoxville was at the head of navigation of the Tennessee River. That alone made it important. But Knoxville also sat astride the most direct rail link between the Confederate capital of Richmond and that part of the Confederacy west of the Appalachian Mountains.

North of Knoxville were mountain passes, which controlled access to Tennessee from Kentucky. With the majority of the population of East Tennessee remaining loyal to the United States, Knoxville was a Confederate island in a sea of Union sympathy.

For almost two years the liberation of East Tennessee from Confederate control had been a dream of the Lincoln Administration. Late summer 1863 found both the favorable conditions and the military imperative necessary to undertake this invasion.

In Kentucky the Union's newest army, the Army of the Ohio, had been assembled under Burnside for the purpose of invading and occupying East Tennessee. In August of 1863 this army swept into the valley, with one of its two corps, the XXIII, marching through the Cumberland Mountains towards Knoxville. The veteran IX Corps slowly returned to Kentucky from service at Vicksburg under General U.S. Grant. It rejoined the Army of the Ohio in Tennessee after a few weeks of recuperation and refitting.

13 November 1863 Longstreet divided his command and sent Wheeler's cavalry across the Little Tennessee River through Rockford to engage Brig. Gen. William E. Sanders's Union cavalry at Maryville. Driving Sanders's cavalry before it, Wheeler's cavalry was ordered to attack Knoxville's southern heights. Sanders, using dismounted cavalry to hold off the Confederate advance from the west, was fatally wounded 18 November 1863. He died the following day.

Longstreet was ordered to march on Knoxville with his First Corps of the Army of Northern Virginia. His orders were to capture or drive out Burnside and the Army of the Ohio. Longstreet's cavalry under Major General Joseph Wheeler was ordered to push through Blount County and attack the heights on the river opposite Knoxville. If the Confederates could capture these heights, Knoxville would be at their mercy.

Meanwhile, to complete the envelopment of Burnside's army, Longstreet's infantry and artillery force assembled a pontoon bridge west of Loudon, crossed the Tennessee River at Huff's Ferry on the night of the 14th, and began a three-day drive, which would bring it to the outskirts of Knoxville and its 15,000 Union defenders. The Confederate siege of Knoxville and the battles to determine its fate were thus begun.

Fort Dickerson was essential in the Union defense of the city. Linking with other hills south of the river, this Union position was a major factor in the defense of Knoxville. The fort and neighboring hills were occupied 1 November 1862 by the 2nd Brig. (Col. Daniel Cameron), 3rd Div., XXIII Corps.

Fort Dickerson was one of sixteen Union Army earthen forts and battery positions protecting Knoxville. It was named for Capt. Jonathan C. Dickerson, 112th Illinois Mounted Infantry, killed near Cleveland, Tennessee, 18 September 1863. Fort Dickerson repulsed assaults by Gen. Wheeler, 15 and 16 November 1863.

The fort also provided artillery support for the battles of Armstrong's Hill, 25 and 29 November 1863.

The Hill, dear to University of Tennessee alumni, was protected by a battery of Federal cannon and a brigade of infantry. A line of entrenchments ran across the west and south slopes.

Fort Sanders was a bastioned earthwork on a ridge two blocks north of U.S. 11 and 16th street. Four brigades of Longstreet's First Corps, emerging from a declivity to the north, made a bayonet charge upon Fort Sanders at dawn 29 November 1863. They were stopped with heavy casualties by a deep ditch.

Bleak House, the home of Robert Houston Armstrong on Kingston Pike in Knoxville, was used as the headquarters of <u>Longstreet</u> and Major Gen. Lafayette McLaws during the siege of Knoxville.

Within hours of the failed assault on Fort Sanders, <u>Longstreet</u> was notified by couriers that Bragg's Army of Tennessee had been defeated by Ulysses S. Grant in the Battle of Missionary Ridge at Chattanooga. With the Confederate army in full retreat, Grant dispatched three Federal columns totaling 25,000 men under the command of Gen. William Tecumseh Sherman to march on Knoxville in relief of <u>Burnside</u>. Knoxville would never be seriously threatened by the Confederates again and remained in Union hands through the end of the war.

Construction of Fort Dickerson was finally completed by the 104th Ohio Battery in February of 1864.

WHEN KIRKSEY LIVED
IN NEW HAVEN

When Kirksey was in graduate school, he played Scrabble with Leon Fleischman. Leon always won. He knew all the little words. Leon ran a liquor store Kirksey could walk to. It was on Whalley Avenue, next to Dino's Pizza.

Kirksey was learning about wine. After a while he would ask Leon for suggestions. "Leon, what's this wine like?"

Leon's answer always was, "Swanny, what can I tell you? Some like it, some don't. We get a lot of repeats."

KIRKSEY AND 1.36 TONS OF #89 STONE

Kirsey drove through the maze at Vulcan Materials in Sevierville. They dumped eleven inches of rock into his pickup bed. So far, so good. But on the spur back to Gatlinburg his truck was waddling, wobbling. It was clearly overloaded. Kirksey was surprised. He had thought his Ford King Ranch was invincible.

But that was only the beginning of his woes. In the driveway of the big house in Gatlinburg he began unloading. What he needed was a magic wand. What he had was a shovel. Three hours later, sunburned and whipped, he looked at the really quite modest pile of rock on the ground. Never again, he swore.

THOUGHTS

SCHIZOPHRENIA AND CERTAINTY

I am heavily vested in my own version of reality. *"My way of analyzing things is the only correct way. That's obvious, right? So here's the deal. Here is what we are going to do."*

My father was a great diagnostician. Perhaps one needs cocksure confidence to pronounce diagnoses. When I was a judge, I had such firm confidence in my legal abilities that I "knew" how a case should be understood and then dealt with. But my twelve law clerks taught me, one after another, that there were other ways than mine to understand a case. I learned that there were creative, different, ways of thinking about the same grist.

Getting to know Mr. X has been mind-changing for me. He had schizophrenia and was "incurable." When I heard of his delusions, I knew he was crazy. End of discussion.

But then, I read his 2008 write-up done by Bertram P. Karon, a psychology professor at Michigan State. The "reality" of Mr. X, was his own valid reality. I learned that it deserved attention, validation, and then, perhaps, some help to guide him back to "our" common, shared Aristotelian reality where a table is a table, an umbrella is an umbrella.

Where the umbrella isn't proof that people are out to get Mr. X.

There is a parallel between the usual psychiatric handling of schizophrenics and what lawyers do in the criminal justice system. Both arenas want their stressors to go away. In psychiatry that means meds and/or electrotherapy--or in the time of Mr. X it meant that. That he has been improperly handled is not even recognized.

A lesser example of this occurs in medicine generally: The patient wants relief, the doctor wants to move on, the patient feels happier if given a drug, any drug, something to walk out with. So the doctor prescribes the drug simply to get rid of the patient.

In the law, the press of the criminal justice docket produces motivation for district attorneys to offer plea compromises. At the outset, the defendant has been multiply charged, often overcharged. *"Throw the book at him."* Then in the negotiation phase, it is suggested that some of the counts will be voluntarily withdrawn, if the defendant will plead to something lesser. The defendant wants his freedom, he has been unable to make bond--or, if able to make bond, he still wants to dispose of the pending charges. So the defendant pleads to something lesser, and gets convicted of the lesser count(s). He has freedom, or a reduced incarceration.

But take the case of the defendant innocent of everything. He has been wrongly arrested. He faces multiple counts, and is urged to accept a lesser plea. He is innocent. He knows it. The likelihood is that he will plead. His attorney does not want him to go to trial. The prosecutor does not want to try the case. The defendant's family wants him back, not risking all on the dice-roll of a trial. So he pleads. In a fair world he would not have been presented with the dilemma.

THE GREEK GODS

In the world of the Greek gods, the world of Homer, individual initiative is a crapshoot. You are the plaything of the gods.

You have been brought up to do offerings, rituals, and pour out fluids. You believe these propitiations are necessary. But the gods are going to do what the gods are going to do regardless.

In the world of Homer, "Man proposes, but it makes no difference." If Zeus or Hera or Athena is calling the shots, you don't run the game.

GEORGE ORWELL'S
1946 WRITING RULES

Before Orwell's 1946 rules, there was William Strunk Jr. (1869-1946).

Strunk first used his own book, *The Elements of Style*, in 1919, privately publishing it for use at Cornell University. Harcourt published it in 1920. Strunk's son Oliver published it again in 1935.

In 1919 E. B. White was a student in Professor Strunk's class at Cornell, where he used "the little book" for himself. Macmillan commissioned him to revise it. White edited the 1959 and 1972 editions of *The Elements of Style*.

In "Politics and the English language," (1946) Orwell teaches:

1. Never use a metaphor, simile or other figure of speech which you are used to seeing in print.
2. Never use a long word where a short one will do.
3. If it is possible to cut a word out, always cut it out.
4. Never use the passive where you can use the active.

5. Never use a foreign phrase, a scientific word or a jargon word if you can think of an everyday English equivalent.
6. Break any of these rules sooner than say anything outright barbarous.

GUNS IN THE USA

The anti-gun lobby uses statistics to make a case against guns: *"Guns in America kill X number of people per year."* Guns are bad; something should be done: *"We must get rid of guns."*

According to the Centers for Disease Control, in 2019 there were 47,511 suicides. Of these, 23,941 were done by firearm. Which is half of all the suicides in the United States.

Ignoring the Second Amendment (which guarantees the right to keep and bear arms), you might believe the anti-gun position is appropriate. You would do this if you believe people should be stopped from killing themselves with guns. If that is your position, well and good. A modern libertarian (but not John Locke) would say the decision for or against suicide is personal. It is not something someone else should decide.

Additionally, there is another question: If guns should somehow be unavailable in the USA, how many of the 23,941 firearm suicides will seek alternate routes?

It is important to bear in mind that the anti-gun lobby's desire to remove guns is **premised on the idea that it can be done**. If the Democrat party somehow achieved a massive penal code for gun possession, then the only persons surrendering guns would be lawful people, most of whom pose no threats to anyone, except perhaps themselves (suicides). All the bad people--and most of the good ones--will keep their guns.

The desire to rid America of guns is also premised on trusting the government:

- to do the removal effectively,
- to protect us from bad guys once we are defenseless,
- and not to oppress us (Venezuela, Cuba, USSR, the Third Reich, Big Brother)

I would love to trust the government. The founding fathers did not. They believed an armed populace was the last protection against an oppressive government.

Let us remember that in 1935 Hitler spoke for his own government about guns: *"This year will go down in history. For the first time, a civilized nation has full gun registration. Our streets will be safer, our police more efficient, and the world will follow our lead into the future!"*

JANICE JOPLIN: DEAD AT TWENTY-EIGHT

Janis Lyn Joplin (January 19, 1943 – October 4, 1970) was an American singer-songwriter who sang rock, soul, and blues music. She was noted for powerful mezzo-soprano vocal and "electric" stage presence.

Joplin was born in Port Arthur, Texas. She had two younger siblings. The family attended First Christian Church of Port Arthur, a church belonging to the Disciples of Christ.

Joplin stated she was ostracized and bullied in high school. She was overweight and suffered from acne, with scars that required dermabrasion. Classmates called her "pig," "freak," "nigger lover," or "creep." She said, "I was a misfit. I read, I painted, I thought. I didn't hate niggers."

In 1963, Joplin was arrested in San Francisco for shoplifting. She was using drugs. During the two years that followed, her drug use increased. She acquired a reputation as a "speed freak" and occasional heroin user. She also was a heavy drinker. Her favorite alcoholic beverage was Southern Comfort.

Joplin appeared at Woodstock 17 August 1969. She and the band were flown by helicopter with the pregnant Joan Baez and Baez's mother from a nearby motel to the festival site. Joplin saw the crowd and became nervous. She was approached by reporters. She referred them to her friend and sometime lover Peggy Caserta.

Joplin was repeatedly delayed by bands contractually obliged to perform ahead of her. Faced with a ten-hour wait after arriving at the backstage area, Joplin spent some of that time shooting heroin and drinking alcohol with Caserta. The director's cut of the Woodstock movie shows Joplin and Jefferson Airplane singer Grace Slick standing together near amplifiers watching Canned Heat's performance.

When Joplin finally reached the stage at 2:00 a.m., she was "three sheets to the wind", according to biographer Alice Echols. During her performance, Joplin's voice was hoarse and wheezy, and she struggled to dance.

Five singles by Joplin reached the *Billboard* Hot 100, including a cover of the Kris Kristofferson song "Me and Bobby McGee". Her most popular songs include cover versions of "Piece of My Heart", "Cry Baby", "Down on Me", "Ball and Chain", and "Summertime". Her only original song was "Mercedes Benz", her final recording.

Joplin died of a heroin overdose at age twenty-eight. She remains one of the top-selling musicians in the United States, with Recording Industry Association of America certifications of 18.5 million albums sold.

BILLY JOEL: MOVIN' OUT

This is a song about capitalism.

> *Anthony works in the grocery store*
> *Saving his pennies for some day.*
> *Mama Leone left a note on the door.*
> *She said, "Sonny, move out to the country."*
> *Oh, but working too hard can give you a heart attack.*
> *You ought to know by now.*
> *Who needs a house out in Hackensack?*
> *Is that all you get for your money?*

Billy Joel does not go on to say what our proper goals should be. If not a house in Hackensack or a Cadillac, then what? His other big hit, *Piano Man,* is no help, because it is also a criticism of shallow living.

However, he is much in favor of intercourse. That is clear. Speaking about *Only the Good Die Young,* he said, "When I wrote *Only the Good Die Young*, the point of the song wasn't so much anti-Catholic as pro-lust. The minute they banned it, the album started shooting up the charts."

LANGUAGE 1: IF YOU CAN SEE IT, YOU CAN SAY IT

One of the good things about German and Spanish is that if you have the written word, you can pronounce it. The pronunciation is absolutely reliable.

Not so in French. If you can see it, you can only maybe say it. Additionally, the French language is famously ambiguous. It is said that is why French is the language of diplomacy.

Now in English, it is sadly <u>not</u> true that you can say it just by looking at the written word. It is often true. It is true often enough to mislead you, but there are daunting exceptions. Consider:

"Cough," where the vowel sound rhymes with "off"
"Enough," where the vowel sound rhymes with "fluff"
"Bough," (of a tree), and "Slough," (muddy wet place, or figuratively, a slough of despond), where the vowel sound rhymes with "cow"
"Through," where the vowel sound rhymes with "goo"
"Thought," where the vowel sound rhymes with "hot"
"Though," where the vowel sound rhymes with "go"

LANGUAGE 2: VERB PROBLEMS

Children have a tough time. In English there are "strong" verbs, meaning verbs which change their stem vowels as they march through their tenses. They are hard to learn, and children can only learn them by hearing them used correctly over and over:

"Bite, bit, bitten": "Don't bite Johnny." "He bit Johnny yesterday." "He had already bitten Johnny when Sarah came into the room."

"Begin, began, begun": "I can't begin to tell you how grateful I am." "I began to tell her how grateful I was." "I had begun to tell Sarah how grateful I was."

"Sink, sank, sunk": "I sink when I try to swim." "I sank when I began to swim." "I had sunk by the time the lifeguard pulled me out."

"Come, came, come": "Come here, Sarah," Mother called. "Sarah came immediately when Mother called." "Sarah had already come into the room when Johnny began to cry."

"Seek, sought, sought": "I seek the truth." "I sought the truth last week." "I had sought the truth relentlessly."

"Fly, flew, flown": "I do not fly on airplanes now." "I flew on airplanes when I was a child." "I have already flown all I want to. I don't do it any more."

"Take, took, taken": "I take exception to that." "I took exception yesterday." "I had taken exception to that at the beginning of the meeting."

"Fling, flang/flung, flung": "I fling a frisbee." "I flung the frisbee as far as I could." ("Flang" is an alternate, but it is not preferred.) "I had flung the frisbee for an hour when I gave up, exhausted."

"Give, gave, given": "I don't give a fig for that." "I gave that no attention." "I have not given that any thought for years."

"Do, did, done": "I do not like green eggs and ham." "I did not like green eggs and ham yesterday, but now I do." "I have done all I can do about my preferences."

"Am, was, been": This is an absolute swamp, dependent upon the person of the speaker ("I am speaking, you are speaking, he is speaking, they are speaking") and of course dependent on the tense ("I am speaking, I was speaking, I had been speaking.")

"Speak, spoke, spoken": "I speak the truth." "I spoke the truth yesterday." "I had spoken to Sarah long before the incident with Johnny."

There are of course "weak" verbs in English. They do not change their stem vowels. Maybe they don't have the courage:

"Like, liked, liked": "I like you." "I liked you yesterday." "I have liked you for as long as I have known you."

"Cry, cried, cried": "Don't cry so much, Johnny." "Johnny cried and cried. He was inconsolable." "He had cried for over twenty minutes by the time Mother came in." (The "y" here is identical in sound to the "ie," so there is not a stem vowel change here.)

"Argue, argued, argued": "You argue too much." "You argued too much yesterday." "You had argued that point *ad nauseam.*"

"Pull, pulled, pulled": "I pull my weight all the time." "I pulled my weight on the team yesterday." "I had pulled my weight, but the coach still took me out of the game."

What children sometimes do is create their own weak verbs out of strong verbs, saying things such as:

"He bited Johnny."

"He thinked for a long time."

"She gived me her book to look at."

ENGLISH HOMOPHONES

Do not get lost in the terminology of homophones and their linguistic kin–the homographs, homonyms, synonyms, heteronyms, etc. It is a huge morass of terms which can leave you feeling inadequate. There are even Venn diagrams which seek to explain the morass. All of this is unnecessary. The only things to remember are:

a. "homo" means the same
b. "phone" means sound
c. "graph" means writing
d. "nym" means name

If you are armed with those concepts, you can navigate all the foolishness that is written about this overdeveloped linguistic landscape.

Here are a few homophones (things that sound alike):

Rain reign rein
Brake break
Creek creak
Rose rose rows
Paste paced
Sear sere

Deer dear
Bawl ball
Rabbit rabbet
Bust bussed
Trust trussed
Mussed must
Tail tale
Sail sale
Pain pane
Bore boar
Reek wreak
Wrought rot
Whore hoar
Their there they're

The list could go on and on. There is even a website which lists the twenty-five homophones most important for non-native English speakers.

SPEAKING LOCAL REVISITED

In my 2021 book "Kirksey" I looked at some local sayings. As time has passed since writing that book, even more localisms have turned up. Here are some of them.

"He was real keerful on the chance they was a snake the other side of the log." Keerful = careful. They was = there was.

"Saved my bacon" = rescued me.

"Kindly" = "somewhat" = "kind of"

"I'ze 'ginnin' to think that . . ." = "I was beginning to think that. . ."

"It's daggon/dadgum dry." = "It is really very dry."

"Out the wazoo" = a lot of something. "I have old pennies out the wazoo."

"Puppies" means (aside from immature dogs) simply "things." Combining these two entries, one can hear, "I got them puppies out the wazoo." Which means, "I really have a lot of those things."

"Sell/sale." This is a matter of pronunciation. For many East Tennesseeans the words are pronounced the same. This is unfortunate, and ignorant, but there it is. An item is "for sell" if you want to dispose of it at a price. There is always a giant "Labor Day Sell" advertised by radio and TV. In print, the newspaper does get it right: "Labor Day Sale."

I have not heard it yet, but I imagine some day I will hear, "The sellboat has two masts."

"I ain't seed bear one for five months." = "I haven't seen any bears at all for five months." "Bear one" is an interesting formulation. It could also be used for any other visible thing, for example, "Chevy one." "I ain't seed Chevrolet one." ("I haven't seen any cars of the Chevrolet brand.")

"Nary," meaning "none." ("I got nary butter. I need to go to the store and get me some.") Nary is an adjective in that sentence. But it can stand alone as a noun: "Have you got any honey left? I got nary."

"Listen atcha" means, "Just listen to you." (An expression of wonderment)

"Hink": "I walk well with two trekking poles, but with only one I just hink along." (Hink is an old word, probably of Scandinavian origin; akin to Old Norse *hinkr*, hesitation, from *hinka* to limp; Middle Low German *hinken*; Old English *hincian*, to limp; Old High German *hinkan*, to limp; Old Norse *skakkr*, crooked, askew.)

"I'm over it." = "I've had enough of this." "I'm done with it." "I am disgusted."

"Not perzackly" = not exactly

"Don't knows I can do it," (and "don't knows as how I can do it") mean, "I am not sure I can do it."

"That's a mite precarious." = A bit risky.

"I've gotta splinker in my thumb." Splinker = splinter. "I have a splinter in my thumb."

"I'm gonna kill me some yellow jackets." What is interesting in this statement is "me," in the dative case. It is an indirect object of the transitive verb "kill." The dative in this construction is often called the dative of advantage or disadvantage, denoting the person or thing for whose benefit or to whose prejudice the action is performed. It occurs in both Latin and German.

"He'll turn you ever' which way but loose." = "You are never going to get shet of him."

"Shet" = shed = "rid of"

"Mad as a wet hen," is commonly said, and you would think that it must describe reality. It doesn't. My hens wander around in the rain even when they could be dry inside their house.

"Purt near" = pretty near; almost

"That wadn't bad." = "That was pretty good." Here the negative is used to yield a positive.

"Gwine to do": "I'm gwine to do that, first chanct I git."

"Crooked as a snake" = "extremely dishonest"

"Roon" = ruin. Roon is used as a verb, never as a noun. "If'n you put your sharp knives in the dishwasher, it'll roon 'em."

"Blarey" = "blurry" This word may be a combination of "glare" and "blur."

"That's just mizzibl." = "That is simply miserable, really too bad, regrettable."

"I'm gone kick yo' ass." The word "gone" here rhymes with tone, bone, and cone. "Gone" = gonna = going to.

"As slick as owl grease" = extremely excellent. The expression is popular throughout the South, but possibly originated in Texas. "Alcalde oil is as slick as owl grease" was cited in Texas newspapers in 1894. A 1931 list of questions about popular expressions asked, "How slick is owl grease?"

"Fast as greased lightning" means simply extremely fast.

"Crazy as a jaybird" = extremely crazy

"Right smuck in the middle" "Smuck" here is used alternatively to "smack." Both the words mean "exactly in the middle."

"Getting nowhere fast" = making no progress, spinning your wheels in the sand

"They seen you comin'" means, "They knew they could take advantage of you, so they fleeced you."

To "fleece someone" is to take his money. An example is the "fish" in a poker game, the guy who is invited because he is known to lose.

"Not worth a tinker's damn" There is disagreement regarding the spelling. Some claim it is *tinker's dam* while others say it should be *tinker's damn*. A tinker travels from one place to another repairing small things like utensils. An early definition of *tinker's dam*, recorded in the year 1877, stated that a tinker's dam was a piece of doughy material that tinkers used to hold metal in place when repairing it. The idea was that this material was worthless once the repair was complete, since it couldn't be reused and could serve no alternative purpose. However, other early versions of this idiom include *a tinker's curse* and *a tinker's cuss*. Apparently, back when being a tinker was a common profession, there was a stereotype that tinkers cursed often. If so, then the severity or importance of each curse would be small.

"All swole up": "He was all swole up from them bee stangs." *Swole* has existed in English since at least the early 1900s. It is used as another word for *swelled* or *swollen*. This is generally used when a part of someone's body has swelled from some type of affliction. This could be from allergies, toxins, being beaten up, or other causes.

"Sep'n I could" = "This is going to be hard to do, sep'n I could do it t'other way round." ("If I do the other way, it will be easy.")

"Tard" = tired

"Truck with" = have to do with. "I'll have no truck with that nonsense."

"Bassackwards" = ass backwards; doing something the wrong way

"Out of kilter" = askew. "There's something out of kilter here."

"Hellacious" = extremely, awfully. "This is hellacious good chili."

"Tarnation" = damnation, hell. Usually with "in." "What in tarnation were you thinking?"

"Gumpshun" = gumption = courage

"Cattywampus" = crooked, out of kilter

"Piss poor" = extremely poor

"A pot to piss in": "He was so poor he didn't have a pot to piss in." This phrase may go back to the times of chamber pots.

"You're pissin' out." This means, "You are giving up, have lost your motivation, you are tired." It does not mean to urinate in the outward direction.

"Piss off!" is an exclamation meaning, "Get lost, go away, don't bother me."

To be "pissed off" is a condition of vexation.

Skeezix: an imaginary body part. "Be careful or you'll break your skeezix."

"Summer's": "It's here summer's." = "It is here somewhere."

"A piece of work": a fool, a person out of step. "He is a piece of work."

"A mort of trouble" = a lot of trouble. "Mort" means a great number, and was first used as such in 1694.

"Sucking wind" = accomplishing nothing, being out of luck. This saying probably derives from the anatomical pneumothorax.

"Fit to be tied": frustrated, upset, out of options

"Fine as frog hair" means extremely excellent. It has nothing to do with the thinness of the filaments.

"Let's nail it." = "Let's do it, let's get it done."

"Auint and Airnt" are guttural sounds. They mean, "All right, OK, what's next, so?"

"Puckerbrush = scrubby bushes, thin bushes

"Front/back stoop" = a small porch. It comes from Middle Dutch.

"I flang it." = "I flung it." The Oxford English Dictionary notes "flang" as a dialectical past tense for fling.

"All tuckered out" = very tired: "I was real tard."

"I ran 'til my tongue was hangin out." = "I ran until I was exhausted." This may come from observing dogs.

"Damnfool" is pronounced the same way as "Coldbeer": The emphasis must be on the first syllable.

"Positively whipped" means completely whipped, completely tired out. It does not mean improved by the experience of whipping.

"Nekkid as a jaybird" means stark naked. But jays are never naked, so this is inexplicable.

Raining sideways: "It was raining to beat the band."

"Gullywasher": "It was raining like a cow pissin' on a flat rock."

"He thought he'd died and gone to heaven." = He believed himself extremely successful.

"Hunkered down": having taken shelter

"They flat whipped us": They completely whipped us. "Flat" is an intensifier.

"Well, I'll be" is an expression of mild amazement.

"Fandangled" = complicated, needlessly complex

"A New York minute" means very quickly. "If they are giving out free tickets, I'll be there in a New York minute."

"Persnickety" = fussy, overly particular

"A country mile" is a phrase meaning a great distance, or simply a lot. "They lost the game by a country mile."

"A fur piece" is a great distance. "Hit's a fur piece from here." A fur piece is less than a country mile.

"In high cotton" = a good condition, a privileged state of being. Picking high cotton was easier than bending down to pick the bolls.

"He ain't right" means he is mentally defective. It does not mean he is incorrect.

"Hit don't make no never mind." = "Don't concern yourself with that." ("These are not the droids you are looking for.")

"Peckerwood" = a fool. The American Heritage Dictionary says "peckerwood" is a Southern U.S. term for a woodpecker, which may well be so, but the dominant use in my experience is to name someone a fool.

"Get on down the road" means to move along, make progress, or simply to leave.

"Mighty perticklr" means overly particular, fussy.

"I'll study on it" means, "I will think about it."

"I might could if'n I tried real hard," means that I might be able to do it, if I seriously applied myself to the project.

"Colder than shit" = extremely cold. Which is absurd, because the temperature of feces is 98.6 degrees Fahrenheit.

"How 'bout them apples?" simply means, "What about that?" It can also be a mild request for the listener to comment.

"That ain't much punkin" = not very good.

"A rank stranger" is a complete stranger, an absolute stranger.

"He squoze into that little tiny space." This is an example of a creative past tense. It is unknown to the Oxford English Dictionary, the American Heritage Dictionary, and Webster's Unabridged. "Squeeze" is an example of what philologists call a "weak" verb, meaning a verb which does not change its stem vowel as its tenses change: "I squeeze the tube of paste today. I squeezed it yesterday. I have squeezed it many times."

"He don't know up from down" is a local way of saying that a fellow is dense or stupid.

"That dog don't hunt," means that something is a bad idea, incorrect, false.

"I turned it over in my head," means that I thought about it.

"Hurtin' fer certain" means definitely hurting (as in pain), but more often it means being at a disability or disadvantage.

"Plumb certain" means definitely certain, as correct and straight as a plumb line.

"I can't splain it no other way" occurs often. It is simply an elision of the first syllable.

"What's the dang deal?" = "What's that all about?"

"Dickhead" is a gross term for a fool. But it can also be a mild term of endearment.

"Shut yo' mouf" is a rude way to tell someone to be quiet.

SAYINGS

"Humble pie" is a figurative serving of humiliation, usually in the form of a forced submission, apology, or retraction. It is often used in the phrase "eat humble pie."

"Up to snuff" means "satisfactory." The origins of the saying are confused, but all related to powdered tobacco inhaled up the nose.

"Air in a jug": "I wouldn't give Yale University air in a jug." More commonly it is used for a person: "I wouldn't give him air in a jug." (Meaning, "I think that little of him.")

"Come a cropper" = "take a heavy fall" To suffer a collapse, crash, defeat, failure, fizzle, nonachievement, nonsuccess.

"Since God was a child" = for a long time right up to the present. "I haven't heard from you since God was a child."

"Like mushrooms after a spring rain" means that something has appeared unexpectedly in great abundance.

"To hector" means to bully someone. However, the original Hector of Homer's *Iliad* was not a bully. He was the eldest son of King Priam of Troy, a model soldier, son, father, and friend, the champion of the Trojan army until killed by the Greek hero Achilles. How did the name of a Trojan paragon become today's generic synonym of *bully*? That pejorative English use was likely influenced by gangs of rowdy street toughs who roamed London in the 17th century and called themselves "Hectors." They thought themselves gallant young blades, but to the general populace they were swaggering bullies who intimidated passersby and vandalized property. By 1660, "hector" was being used as a noun for the sort of blustering braggarts who populated those gangs, and as a verb as well. In the *Iliad,* the counterpart to Hector is Nestor. He was the eldest of the Greek leaders in the Trojan War. He had been a great warrior as a young man, but in the *Iliad* he is noted chiefly for his wisdom and talkativeness, both of which increased as he aged. These days, a nestor is not necessarily long-winded, but merely wise and generous with his advice. A second meaning of a nestor today is a patriarch or leader in a field.

"It is high time" means something is overdue to happen, that it is time that it occur. In German, the phrase is "höchste Zeit": "Es ist ja höchste Zeit, dass du nach Hause kommst."

"Thou shalt not muzzle the ox that treads thy grain" is biblical, from Deuteronomy 25:4. The point is that the laborer is worthy of his hire. 1 Corinthians 9:9.

"Hand over fist" = rapidly, quickly. This is believed to come from a sailor's hauling in of a rope rapidly, hand over hand.

"Cry uncle," a call by one child for another to submit or cry for mercy. It appears variously as *say uncle!, cry uncle!* or *holler uncle!* First recorded in print in the US early in the twentieth century.

"Like a redheaded stepchild": out of the gene pool, out of place, a child who is obviously not your own, a child who is treated worse than other children in the family. Particularly in noble circles, the presence of a stepchild or illegitimate child posed a threat to inheritance. Shakespeare used the illegitimate child (Edmund the Bastard in *King Lear*, John the Bastard in *Much Ado About Nothing*). *Snow White* and *Cinderella* stress conflict between stepparents and stepchildren.

"To beat the band" = extremely: "It was raining to beat the band."

"Going nowhere fast" = "spinning your wheels" = "What you are engaged in is futile."

"I didn't know him from Adam's off ox." The "Grammarist" website says that "I *don't know him from Adam's off ox"* *means* the speaker is a stranger to him. An "off ox" is the draft animal in a team situated on the right, farthest from the driver. The driver places the most experienced draft animal closest to his guiding leads, hoping the off ox will simply follow what the lead animal does. The off ox often does not have the best footing in a situation, and may stumble. Also, the off ox is not as prized as the near ox, and the idiom "poor as Adam's off ox" was popular for a while. Other regionalisms embellishing the original phrase include *don't know someone from Adam's house cat,* and *don't know someone from Adam's grandmother.* Though the idiom "don't know someone from Adam's off ox" has been in use since at least the latter 1880s. It did not emerge into popular culture until Bill Clinton used the term in the 1990s.

"My stomach thinks my throat's cut" means simply, "I am very hungry."

"Damn straight" = "absolutely"

"Quiet as a mouse" = very quiet. "And all through the house, not a creature was stirring, not even a mouse."

"Deaf as a post" dates from the 16th century. It is first recorded in *The Comedye of Acolastus* (1540) by John Palsgrave. Obviously, there is little point in talking to a wooden post.

"The cat's meow" = the epitome, perfection. "She thought she was just the cat's meow." Very appealing: "I really like that car; it's the cat's meow."

"Silly goose" refers to a person who acts in a childish, foolish, somewhat comical way. This term originates from several sources. Brewer's *Dictionary of Phrase and Fable* states, "A foolish or ignorant person is called a goose because of the alleged stupidity of this bird."

"Couldn't hear yourself think" = "There was so much noise I was unable to form thoughts."

"Dead to rights" is referred to in the *Dictionary of Clichés* by Christine Ammer as "being absolutely without doubt; also, red-handed, in the act of doing something." The term originated in the United States in the mid-nineteenth century and was used mostly with criminal activity. In 1859 George Washington Marsell defined it in his *Vocabulum* (also called

The Rogue's Lexicon) as "positively guilty with no way of getting clear."

"Standoffish" is said of a detached or reserved person, for example a person who avoids eye contact and doesn't talk with people in a group setting.

"Dead as a doornail" = definitely deceased. *"Old Marley was as dead as a door-nail. Mind! I don't mean to say that I know, of my own knowledge, what there is particularly dead about a door-nail. I might have been inclined, myself, to regard a coffin-nail as the deadest piece of ironmongery in the trade. But the wisdom of our ancestors is in the simile; and my unhallowed hands shall not disturb it, or the Country's done for. You will therefore permit me to repeat, emphatically, that Marley was as dead as a door-nail."*

"Sweet as pie" = Particularly sweet, friendly, or kindly. "The kids may be sweet as pie right now, but they can be little terrors when they want to be."

"Suck-up"= ass kisser, brown noser. "He was a suck-up."

"A stick in the mud" is a person who is slow, old-fashioned, unprogressive; an old fogey.

"Spoilsport" = One who mars the pleasure of others. Someone who puts an end to others' fun, especially harmless fun.

"Had me/got me by the short hairs" = To acquire complete control, dominance, or power over someone, especially in a difficult or awkward situation.

"Frightened/scared me out of my wits" means "afraid, fearful, nervous, panicky, agitated, alarmed, worried, intimidated."

"At my wits' end" means "So worried, confused, or annoyed that I do not know what to do next."

"Topsy-turvy" = in utter confusion or disorder; also, with the top or head downward. Upside down.

Sad sack = a blundering, inept person. Additionally, "Sad Sack" was an American World War II comic strip and comic book character of George Baker, who depicted an otherwise unnamed, lowly private experiencing absurdities and humiliations in military life. (The title was a euphemistic shortening of the military slang "sad sack of shit", common during World War II.)

"I did it on a lark" means to do something on a whim or just for fun. "On a lark we diverted our journey from Rome to Amsterdam." A lark, in British slang, is a gag or a joke. The phrase "on a lark" is then something done as a joke.

"What the Sam Hill!" is American English slang. It is a euphemism or minced oath for "the devil" or "hell." ("What in the Sam Hill is that?") According to the Oxford English Dictionary it is of unknown origin. Etymologist Michael Quinion and others date the expression back to the late 1830s; they and others consider it a simple bowdlerization. (To "bowdlerize" is to remove material that is considered offensive or objectionable.) Thomas Bowdler, 1754-1825, was an English physician who published *The Family Shakespeare*, an expurgated edition of Shakespeare's plays. He sought a version more appropriate than the original for 19th-century women and children.

"Shot my wad" comes from the days of musket guns, where a wad (strips of cloth) was packed down the barrel to create a seal between the gunpowder and the bullet, increasing the internal pressure when the gunpowder fired, and thus speeding the bullet. Today, it can mean to lose or spend all one's money. "My Las Vegas trip was short lived. I shot my wad at the poker table in the first two hours!" Also vulgar slang for "to ejaculate semen."

"Hokum" is a device to evoke a desired audience response. It is pretentious nonsense, "bunkum." Something apparently impressive or legitimate but actually untrue or insincere; nonsense.

"Pull my leg" = to tease or fool someone; to trick someone in a humorous way. (This term for a time was thought to allude to the practice of pulling on the legs of a person being hanged in order to shorten the agony.)

THE GERMAN BLUE TICKPICKER REVISITED

After another viewing of the mockumentary *"Best in Show,"* I cannot resist publishing this small piece once more.

A script for the announcer of the Westminster Dog Show:

The German Blue Tick Picker is a dog with a long and difficult ancestry. From earliest times it has had few friends. Self-possessed, it will not hunt, herd, or retrieve--steadfastly resisting all efforts at utility. The German Blue Tick Picker exists today solely because of his striking devotion to procreation.

Not friendly to children, the Tick Picker requires a great deal of open space for its rambunctious nature. With a matted and twisted coat, the Tick Picker requires daily grooming. This is a dog which gets along best with a servile master.

Despite its name, the German Blue Tick Picker is not picky about food, and will eat almost anything.

The German Blue Tick Picker, number 8.

HANSEL AND GRETEL

I have written about the brothers Grimm before: in my 2021 *Kirksey* ("How the Children Played Butchering with Each Other"). To understate the situation, the Grimms did not sanitize what they collected from the German landscape of oral tradition, no matter how horrible the content. Disney of course did, and you can be of two minds about that. All in all, it is probably better to wait for adulthood before learning the truth about Cinderella, about Snow White, and about Hansel and Gretel's wicked stepmother and their devoted but feckless father.

Judge for yourself:

Hänsel und Gretel

Hansel and Gretel

Vor einem großen Walde wohnte ein armer Holzhacker mit seiner Frau und seinen zwei Kindern; das Bübchen hieß Hänsel und das Mädchen Gretel. Er hatte wenig zu beißen und zu brechen, und einmal, als große Teuerung ins Land kam, konnte er das tägliche Brot nicht mehr schaffen.

Wie er sich nun abends im Bette Gedanken machte und sich vor Sorgen herumwälzte, seufzte er und sprach zu seiner Frau: "Was soll aus uns werden? Wie können wir unsere armen Kinder ernähren da wir für uns selbst nichts mehr haben?" -

"Weißt du was, Mann," antwortete die Frau, "wir wollen morgen in aller Frühe die Kinder hinaus in den Wald führen, wo er am dicksten ist. Da machen wir ihnen ein Feuer an und geben jedem noch ein Stückchen Brot, dann gehen wir an unsere Arbeit und lassen sie allein. Sie finden den Weg nicht wieder nach Haus, und wir sind sie los." -

"Nein, Frau," sagte der Mann, "das tue ich nicht; wie sollt ich's übers Herz bringen, meine Kinder im Walde allein zu lassen! Die wilden Tiere würden bald kommen und sie zerreißen." - "Oh, du Narr," sagte sie, "dann müssen wir alle viere Hungers sterben, du kannst nur die Bretter für die Särge hobeln," und ließ ihm keine Ruhe, bis er einwilligte. "Aber die armen Kinder dauern mich doch," sagte der Mann.

Die zwei Kinder hatten vor Hunger auch nicht einschlafen können und hatten gehört, was die Stiefmutter zum Vater gesagt hatte. Gretel weinte bittere Tränen und sprach zu Hänsel: "Nun ist's um uns geschehen." -

Near by a great forest dwelt a poor wood-cutter with his wife and his two children. The boy was called Hansel and the girl Gretel. He had little to bite and to break, and once when great famine fell on the land, he could no longer procure even daily bread.

Now when he thought this over by night in his bed, and tossed about in his anxiety, he groaned and said to his wife: 'What is to become of us? How are we to feed our poor children, when we no longer have anything even for ourselves?'

'I'll tell you what, husband,' answered the woman, 'early tomorrow morning we will take the children out into the forest to where it is the thickest; there we will light a fire for them, and give each of them one more piece of bread, and then we will go to our work and leave them alone. They will not find the way home again, and we shall be rid of them.'

'No, wife,' said the man, 'I will not do that; how can I bear to leave my children alone in the forest?—the wild animals would soon come and tear them to pieces.' 'O, you fool!' said she, 'then we must all four die of hunger, you may as well plane the planks for our coffins,' and she left him no peace until he consented. 'But I feel very sorry for the poor children, all the same,' said the man.

The two children had also not been able to sleep because of hunger, and had heard what their stepmother had said to their father. Gretel wept bitter tears, and said to Hansel: 'Now all is over with us.'

"Still, Gretel," sprach Hänsel, "gräme dich nicht, ich will uns schon helfen." Und als die Alten eingeschlafen waren, stand er auf, zog sein Röcklein an, machte die Untertüre auf und schlich sich hinaus. Da schien der Mond ganz hell, und die weißen Kieselsteine, die vor dem Haus lagen, glänzten wie lauter Batzen. Hänsel bückte sich und steckte so viele in sein Rocktäschlein, als nur hinein wollten. Dann ging er wieder zurück, sprach zu Gretel: "Sei getrost, liebes Schwesterchen, und schlaf nur ruhig ein, Gott wird uns nicht verlassen," und legte sich wieder in sein Bett.

Als der Tag anbrach, noch ehe die Sonne aufgegangen war, kam schon die Frau und weckte die beiden Kinder: "Steht auf, ihr Faulenzer, wir wollen in den Wald gehen und Holz holen."
Dann gab sie jedem ein Stückchen Brot und sprach: "Da habt ihr etwas für den Mittag, aber eßt's nicht vorher auf, weiter kriegt ihr nichts." Gretel nahm das Brot unter die Schürze, weil Hänsel die Steine in der Tasche hatte. Danach machten sie sich alle zusammen auf den Weg nach dem Wald.

Als sie ein Weilchen gegangen waren, stand Hänsel still und guckte nach dem Haus zurück und tat das wieder und immer wieder. Der Vater sprach: "Hänsel, was guckst du da und bleibst zurück, hab acht und vergiß deine Beine nicht!" -
"Ach, Vater," sagte Hänsel, "ich sehe nach meinem weißen Kätzchen, das sitzt oben auf dem Dach und will mir Ade sagen."
Die Frau sprach: "Narr, das ist dein Kätzchen nicht, das ist die Morgensonne, die auf den Schornstein scheint." Hänsel aber hatte nicht nach dem Kätzchen gesehen, sondern immer einen von den blanken Kieselsteinen aus seiner Tasche auf den Weg geworfen.

'Be quiet, Gretel,' said Hansel, 'do not distress yourself, I will soon find a way to help us.' And when the old folks had fallen asleep, he got up, put on his little coat, opened the door below, and crept outside. The moon shone brightly, and the white pebbles which lay in front of the house glittered like real silver pennies. Hansel stooped and stuffed the little pocket of his coat with as many as he could get in. Then he went back and said to Gretel: 'Be comforted, dear little sister, and sleep in peace, God will not forsake us,' and he lay down again in his bed.

When day dawned, but before the sun had risen, the woman came and awoke the two children, saying: 'Get up, you sluggards! we are going into the forest to fetch wood.'
She gave each a little piece of bread, and said: 'There is something for your dinner, but do not eat it up before then, for you will get nothing else.' Gretel took the bread under her apron, as Hansel had the pebbles in his pocket. Then they all set out together on the way to the forest.

When they had walked a short time, Hansel stood still and peeped back at the house, and did so again and again. His father said: 'Hansel, what are you looking at there and staying behind for? Pay attention, and do not forget how to use your legs.'
'Ah, father,' said Hansel, 'I am looking at my little white cat, which is sitting up on the roof, and wants to say goodbye to me.'
The wife said: 'Fool, that is not your little cat, that is the morning sun which is shining on the chimneys.' Hansel, however, had not been looking back at the cat, but had been constantly throwing one of the white pebble-stones out of his pocket on the road.

Als sie mitten in den Wald gekommen waren, sprach der Vater: "Nun sammelt Holz, ihr Kinder, ich will ein Feuer anmachen, damit ihr nicht friert." Hänsel und Gretel trugen Reisig zusammen, einen kleinen Berg hoch. Das Reisig ward angezündet, und als die Flamme recht hoch brannte, sagte die Frau: "Nun legt euch ans Feuer, ihr Kinder, und ruht euch aus, wir gehen in den Wald und hauen Holz. Wenn wir fertig sind, kommen wir wieder und holen euch ab."

Hänsel und Gretel saßen um das Feuer, und als der Mittag kam, aß jedes sein Stücklein Brot. Und weil sie die Schläge der Holzaxt hörten, so glaubten sie, ihr Vater wär' in der Nähe. Es war aber nicht die Holzaxt, es war ein Ast, den er an einen dürren Baum gebunden hatte und den der Wind hin und her schlug.

Und als sie so lange gesessen hatten, fielen ihnen die Augen vor Müdigkeit zu, und sie schliefen fest ein. Als sie endlich erwachten, war es schon finstere Nacht. Gretel fing an zu weinen und sprach: "Wie sollen wir nun aus dem Wald kommen?" Hänsel aber tröstete sie: "Wart nur ein Weilchen, bis der Mond aufgegangen ist, dann wollen wir den Weg schon finden." Und als der volle Mond aufgestiegen war, so nahm Hänsel sein Schwesterchern an der Hand und ging den Kieselsteinen nach, die schimmerten wie neugeschlagene Batzen und zeigten ihnen den Weg.

Sie gingen die ganze Nacht hindurch und kamen bei anbrechendem Tag wieder zu ihres Vaters Haus. Sie klopften an die Tür, und als die Frau aufmachte und sah, daß es Hänsel und Gretel waren, sprach sie:

When they had reached the middle of the forest, the father said: 'Now, children, pile up some wood, and I will light a fire so that you may not be cold.' Hansel and Gretel gathered brushwood together, as high as a little hill. The brushwood was lit, and when the flames were burning very high, the woman said: 'Now, children, lay yourselves down by the fire and rest, we will go into the forest and cut some wood. When we are done, we will come back and fetch you away.'

Hansel and Gretel sat by the fire, and when noon came, each ate a little piece of bread, and as they heard the strokes of the wood-axe they believed that their father was near. It was not the axe, however, but a branch which he had fastened to a withered tree which the wind was blowing backwards and forwards.

And as they had been sitting for such a long time, their eyes closed with fatigue, and they fell fast asleep. When at last they awoke, it was already dark night. Gretel began to cry and said: 'How are we to get out of the forest now?' But Hansel comforted her and said: 'Just wait a little, until the moon has risen, and then we will soon find the way.' And when the full moon had risen, Hansel took his little sister by the hand, and followed the pebbles which shone like newly-coined silver pieces, and showed them the way.

They walked the whole night long, and by break of day came once more to their father's house. They knocked at the door, and when the woman opened it and saw that it was Hansel and Gretel, she said:

"Ihr bösen Kinder, was habt ihr so lange im Walde geschlafen, wir haben geglaubt, ihr wollet gar nicht wiederkommen." Der Vater aber freute sich, denn es war ihm zu Herzen gegangen, daß er sie so allein zurückgelassen hatte.

Nicht lange danach war wieder Not in allen Ecken, und die Kinder hörten, wie die Mutter nachts im Bette zu dem Vater sprach: "Alles ist wieder aufgezehrt, wir haben noch einen halben Laib Brot, hernach hat das Lied ein Ende. Die Kinder müssen fort, wir wollen sie tiefer in den Wald hineinführen, damit sie den Weg nicht wieder herausfinden; es ist sonst keine Rettung für uns."

Dem Mann fiel's schwer aufs Herz, und er dachte: Es wäre besser, daß du den letzten Bissen mit deinen Kindern teiltest. Aber die Frau hörte auf nichts, was er sagte, schalt ihn und machte ihm Vorwürfe.

Wer A sagt, muß B sagen, und weil er das erstemal nachgegeben hatte, so mußte er es auch zum zweitenmal.

Die Kinder waren aber noch wach gewesen und hatten das Gespräch mitangehört. Als die Alten schliefen, stand Hänsel wieder auf, wollte hinaus und die Kieselsteine auflesen, wie das vorigemal; aber die Frau hatte die Tür verschlossen, und Hänsel konnte nicht heraus. Aber er tröstete sein Schwesterchen und sprach: "Weine nicht, Gretel, und schlaf nur ruhig, der liebe Gott wird uns schon helfen."

Am frühen Morgen kam die Frau und holte die Kinder aus dem Bette. Sie erhielten ihr Stückchen Brot, das war aber noch kleiner als das vorigemal. Auf dem Wege nach dem Wald bröckelte es Hänsel in der Tasche, stand oft still und warf ein Bröcklein auf die Erde.

'You naughty children, why have you slept so long in the forest?—we thought you were never coming back at all!' The father, however, rejoiced, for it had cut him to the heart to leave them behind alone.

Not long afterwards, there was once more great dearth throughout the land, and the children heard their mother saying at night to their father: 'Everything is eaten again, we have one half loaf left, and that is the end. The children must go, we will take them farther into the woods, so that they will not find their way out again; there is no other means of saving ourselves!'

The man's heart was heavy, and he thought: 'It would be better for you to share the last mouthful with your children.' The woman, however, would listen to nothing that he had to say, but scolded and reproached him.

He who says A must say B, likewise, and as he had yielded the first time, he had to do so a second time also.

The children, however, were still awake and had heard the conversation. When the old folks were asleep, Hansel again got up, and wanted to go out and pick up pebbles as he had done before, but the woman had locked the door, and Hansel could not get out. Nevertheless he comforted his little sister, and said: 'Do not cry, Gretel, go to sleep quietly, the good God will help us.'

Early in the morning came the woman, and took the children out of their beds. Their piece of bread was given to them, but it was still smaller than the time before. On the way into the forest Hansel crumbled his in his pocket, and often stood still and threw a morsel on the ground.

"Hänsel, was stehst du und guckst dich um?" sagte der Vater, "geh deiner Wege!" - "Ich sehe nach meinem Täubchen, das sitzt auf dem Dache und will mir Ade sagen," antwortete Hänsel.

'Hansel, why do you stop and look round?' said the father, 'go on.' 'I am looking back at my little pigeon which is sitting on the roof, and wants to say goodbye to me,' answered Hansel.

"Narr," sagte die Frau, "das ist dein Täubchen nicht, das ist die Morgensonne, die auf den Schornstein oben scheint." Hänsel aber warf nach und nach alle Bröcklein auf den Weg.

'Fool!' said the woman, 'that is not your little pigeon, that is the morning sun that is shining on the chimney.' Hansel, however little by little, threw all the crumbs on the path.

Die Frau führte die Kinder noch tiefer in den Wald, wo sie ihr Lebtag noch nicht gewesen waren. Da ward wieder ein großes Feuer angemacht, und die Mutter sagte:

The woman led the children still deeper into the forest, where they had never in their lives been before. Then a great fire was again made, and the mother said:

"Bleibt nur da sitzen, ihr Kinder, und wenn ihr müde seid, könnt ihr ein wenig schlafen. Wir gehen in den Wald und hauen Holz, und abends, wenn wir fertig sind, kommen wir und holen euch ab." Als es Mittag war, teilte Gretel ihr Brot mit Hänsel, der sein Stück auf den Weg gestreut hatte. Dann schliefen sie ein, und der Abend verging; aber niemand kam zu den armen Kindern. Sie erwachten erst in der finstern Nacht, und Hänsel tröstete sein Schwesterchen und sagte: "Wart nur, Gretel, bis der Mond aufgeht, dann werden wir die Brotbröcklein sehen, die ich ausgestreut habe, die zeigen uns den Weg nach Haus." Als der Mond kam, machten sie sich auf, aber sie fanden kein Bröcklein mehr, denn die viel tausend Vögel, die im Walde und im Felde umherfliegen, die hatten sie weggepickt.

'Just sit there, you children, and when you are tired you may sleep a little; we are going into the forest to cut wood, and in the evening when we are done, we will come and fetch you away.' When it was noon, Gretel shared her piece of bread with Hansel, who had scattered his by the way. Then they fell asleep and evening passed, but no one came to the poor children. They did not awake until it was dark, and Hansel comforted his little sister and said: 'Just wait, Gretel, until the moon rises, and then we shall see the crumbs of bread which I have strewn about, they will show us our way home again.' When the moon came they set out, but they found no crumbs, for the many thousands of birds which fly about in the woods and fields had pecked them all up.

Hänsel sagte zu Gretel: "Wir werden den Weg schon finden." Aber sie fanden ihn nicht. Sie gingen die ganze Nacht und noch einen Tag von Morgen bis Abend, aber sie kamen aus dem Wald nicht heraus und waren so hungrig, denn sie hatten nichts als die paar Beeren, die auf der Erde standen. Und weil sie so müde waren, daß die Beine sie nicht mehr tragen wollten, so legten sie sich unter einen Baum und schliefen ein.

Hansel said to Gretel: 'We shall soon find the way,' but they did not find it. They walked the whole night and all the next day too from morning till evening, but they did not get out of the forest, and were very hungry, for they had nothing to eat but two or three berries, which grew on the ground. And as they were so weary that their legs would carry them no longer, they lay down beneath a tree and fell asleep.

Nun war's schon der dritte Morgen, daß sie ihres Vaters Haus verlassen hatten. Sie fingen wieder an zu gehen, aber sie gerieten immer tiefer in den Wald, und wenn nicht bald Hilfe kam, mußten sie verschmachten.

Als es Mittag war, sahen sie ein schönes, schneeweißes Vögelein auf einem Ast sitzen, das sang so schön, daß sie stehen blieben und ihm zuhörten. Und als es fertig war, schwang es seine Flügel und flög vor ihnen her, und sie gingen ihm nach, bis sie zu einem Häuschen gelangten, auf dessen Dach es sich setzte, und als sie ganz nahe herankamen, so sahen sie, daß das Häuslein aus Brot gebaut war und mit Kuchen gedeckt; aber die Fenster waren von hellem Zucker.

"Da wollen wir uns dranmachen," sprach Hänsel, "und eine gesegnete Mahlzeit halten. Ich will ein Stück vom Dach essen, Gretel, du kannst vom Fenster essen, das schmeckt süß." Hänsel reichte in die Höhe und brach sich ein wenig vom Dach ab, um zu versuchen, wie es schmeckte, und Gretel stellte sich an die Scheiben und knupperte daran.

Da rief eine feine Stimme aus der Stube heraus: "Knupper, knupper, Kneischen, Wer knuppert an meinem Häuschen?"

Die Kinder antworteten: "Der Wind, der Wind, Das himmlische Kind," und aßen weiter, ohne sich irre machen zu lassen. Hänsel, dem das Dach sehr gut schmeckte, riß sich ein großes Stück davon herunter, und Gretel stieß eine ganze runde Fensterscheibe heraus, setzte sich nieder und tat sich wohl damit. Da ging auf einmal die Türe auf, und eine steinalte Frau, die sich auf eine Krücke stützte, kam herausgeschlichen.

It was now three mornings since they had left their father's house. They began to walk again, but they always came deeper into the forest, and if help did not come soon, they would die of hunger and weariness.

When it was mid-day, they saw a beautiful snow-white bird sitting on a bough, which sang so delightfully that they stood still and listened to it. And when its song was over, it spread its wings and flew away before them, and they followed it until they reached a little house, on the roof of which it alighted; and when they approached the little house they saw that it was built of bread and covered with cakes, but that the windows were of clear sugar.

'We will set to work on that,' said Hansel, 'and have a good meal. I will eat a bit of the roof, and you Gretel, can eat some of the window, it will taste sweet.' Hansel reached up above, and broke off a little of the roof to try how it tasted, and Gretel leant against the window and nibbled at the panes.

Then a soft voice cried from the parlour: 'Nibble, nibble, gnaw, Who is nibbling at my little house?'

The children answered: 'The wind, the wind, The heaven-born wind,' and went on eating without disturbing themselves. Hansel, who liked the taste of the roof, tore down a great piece of it, and Gretel pushed out the whole of one round window-pane, sat down, and enjoyed herself with it. Suddenly the door opened, and a woman as old as the hills, who supported herself on crutches, came creeping out.

Hänsel und Gretel erschraken so gewaltig, daß sie fallen ließen, was sie in den Händen hielten. Die Alte aber wackelte mit dem Kopfe und sprach: "Ei, ihr lieben Kinder, wer hat euch hierher gebracht? Kommt nur herein und bleibt bei mir, es geschieht euch kein Leid." Sie faßte beide an der Hand und führte sie in ihr Häuschen. Da ward ein gutes Essen aufgetragen, Milch und Pfannkuchen mit Zucker, Äpfel und Nüsse. Hernach wurden zwei schöne Bettlein weiß gedeckt, und Hänsel und Gretel legten sich hinein und meinten, sie wären im Himmel.

Die Alte hatte sich nur freundlich angestellt, sie war aber eine böse Hexe, die den Kindern auflauerte, und hatte das Brothäuslein bloß gebaut, um sie herbeizulocken. Wenn eins in ihre Gewalt kam, so machte sie es tot, kochte es und aß es, und das war ihr ein Festtag. Die Hexen haben rote Augen und können nicht weit sehen, aber sie haben eine feine Witterung wie die Tiere und merken's, wenn Menschen herankommen. Als Hänsel und Gretel in ihre Nähe kamen, da lachte sie boshaft und sprach höhnisch:

Hansel and Gretel were so terribly frightened that they let fall what they had in their hands. The old woman, however, nodded her head, and said: 'Oh, you dear children, who has brought you here? do come in, and stay with me. No harm shall happen to you.' She took them both by the hand, and led them into her little house. Then good food was set before them, milk and pancakes, with sugar, apples, and nuts. Afterwards two pretty little beds were covered with clean white linen, and Hansel and Gretel lay down in them, and thought they were in heaven.

The old woman had only pretended to be so kind; she was in reality a wicked witch, who lay in wait for children, and had only built the little house of bread in order to entice them there. When a child fell into her power, she killed it, cooked and ate it, and that was a feast day with her. Witches have red eyes, and cannot see far, but they have a keen scent like the beasts, and are aware when human beings draw near. When Hansel and Gretel came into her neighbourhood, she laughed with malice, and said mockingly:

"Die habe ich, die sollen mir nicht wieder entwischen!" Früh morgens, ehe die Kinder erwacht waren, stand sie schon auf, und als sie beide so lieblich ruhen sah, mit den vollen roten Backen, so murmelte sie vor sich hin: "Das wird ein guter Bissen werden."
Da packte sie Hänsel mit ihrer dürren Hand und trug ihn in einen kleinen Stall und sperrte ihn mit einer Gittertüre ein.

Er mochte schrein, wie er wollte, es half ihm nichts. Dann ging sie zur Gretel, rüttelte sie wach und rief:
"Steh auf, Faulenzerin, trag Wasser und koch deinem Bruder etwas Gutes, der sitzt draußen im Stall und soll fett werden.

Wenn er fett ist, so will ich ihn essen."
Gretel fing an bitterlich zu weinen; aber es war alles vergeblich, sie mußte tun, was die böse Hexe verlangte.

Nun ward dem armen Hänsel das beste Essen gekocht, aber Gretel bekam nichts als Krebsschalen. Jeden Morgen schlich die Alte zu dem Ställchen und rief:
"Hänsel, streck deine Finger heraus, damit ich fühle, ob du bald fett bist."
Hänsel streckte ihr aber ein Knöchlein heraus, und die Alte, die trübe Augen hatte, konnte es nicht sehen und meinte, es wären Hänsels Finger, und verwunderte sich, daß er gar nicht fett werden wollte.
Als vier Wochen herum waren und Hänsel immer mager blieb, da überkam sie die Ungeduld, und sie wollte nicht länger warten.
"Heda, Gretel," rief sie dem Mädchen zu, "sei flink und trag Wasser! Hänsel mag fett oder mager sein, morgen will ich ihn schlachten und kochen."
Ach, wie jammerte das arme Schwesterchen, als es das Wasser tragen mußte, und wie flossen ihm die Tränen über die Backen herunter!

'I have them, they shall not escape me again!' Early in the morning before the children were awake, she was already up, and when she saw both of them sleeping and looking so pretty, with their plump and rosy cheeks she muttered to herself: 'That will be a dainty mouthful!' Then she seized Hansel with her shrivelled hand, carried him into a little stall, and locked him in behind a grated door.

Scream as he might, it would not help him. Then she went to Gretel, shook her till she awoke, and cried:
'Get up, lazy thing, fetch some water, and cook something good for your brother, he is in the stall outside, and is to be made fat.

When he is fat, I will eat him.' Gretel began to weep bitterly, but it was all in vain, for she was forced to do what the wicked witch commanded.

And now the best food was cooked for poor Hansel, but Gretel got nothing but crab-shells. Every morning the woman crept to the little stable, and cried: 'Hansel, stretch out your finger so that I may feel if you will soon be fat.' Hansel, however, stretched out a little bone to her, and the old woman, who had dim eyes, could not see it, and thought it was Hansel's finger, and was astonished that there was no way of fattening him.
When four weeks had gone by, and Hansel still remained thin, she was seized with impatience and would not wait any longer.
'Now, then, Gretel,' she cried to the girl, 'stir yourself, and bring some water. Let Hansel be fat or lean, tomorrow I will kill him, and cook him.'
Ah, how the poor little sister did lament when she had to fetch the water, and how her tears did flow down her cheeks!

"Lieber Gott, hilf uns doch," rief sie aus, "hätten uns nur die wilden Tiere im Wald gefressen, so wären wir doch zusammen gestorben!" -
"Spar nur dein Geplärre," sagte die Alte, "es hilft dir alles nichts."

Frühmorgens mußte Gretel heraus, den Kessel mit Wasser aufhängen und Feuer anzünden.
"Erst wollen wir backen," sagte die Alte, "ich habe den Backofen schon eingeheizt und den Teig geknetet."
Sie stieß das arme Gretel hinaus zu dem Backofen, aus dem die Feuerflammen schon herausschlugen "Kriech hinein," sagte die Hexe, "und sieh zu, ob recht eingeheizt ist, damit wir das Brot hineinschieben können."
Und wenn Gretel darin war, wollte sie den Ofen zumachen und Gretel sollte darin braten, und dann wollte sie's aufessen. Aber Gretel merkte, was sie im Sinn hatte, und sprach:
"Ich weiß nicht, wie ich's machen soll; wie komm ich da hinein?" -
"Dumme Gans," sagte die Alte, "die Öffnung ist groß genug, siehst du wohl, ich könnte selbst hinein," krabbelte heran und steckte den Kopf in den Backofen.
Da gab ihr Gretel einen Stoß, daß sie weit hineinfuhr, machte die eiserne Tür zu und schob den Riegel vor.
Hu! Da fing sie an zu heulen, ganz grauselich; aber Gretel lief fort, und die böse Frau mußte elendiglich verbrennen.

Gretel aber lief schnurstracks zum Hänsel, öffnete sein Ställchen und rief: "Hänsel, wir sind erlöst, die alte Hexe ist tot."

Da sprang Hänsel heraus wie ein Vogel aus dem Käfig, wenn ihm die Türe aufgemacht wird. Wie haben sie sich gefreut sind sich um den Hals gefallen, sind herumgesprungen und haben sich geküßt!

'Dear God, do help us,' she cried. 'If the wild beasts in the forest had but devoured us, we should at any rate have died together.'
'Just keep your noise to yourself,' said the old woman, 'it won't help you at all.'

Early in the morning, Gretel had to go out and hang up the cauldron with the water, and light the fire.
'We will bake first,' said the old woman, 'I have already heated the oven, and kneaded the dough.'
She pushed poor Gretel out to the oven, from which flames of fire were already darting. 'Creep in,' said the witch, 'and see if it is properly heated, so that we can put the bread in.'

And once Gretel was inside, she intended to shut the oven and let her bake in it, and then she would eat her, too. But Gretel saw what she had in mind, and said:
'I do not know how I am to do it; how do I get in?'
'Silly goose,' said the old woman. 'The door is big enough; just look, I can get in myself!' and she crept up and thrust her head into the oven.

Then Gretel gave her a push that drove her far into it, and shut the iron door, and fastened the bolt.
Oh! Then she began to howl quite terribly, but Gretel ran away and the evil woman was miserably burnt to death.

Gretel, however, ran like lightning to Hansel, opened his little stall, and cried: 'Hansel, we are saved! The old witch is dead!'

Then Hansel sprang like a bird from its cage when the door is opened. How they did rejoice and embrace each other, and dance about and kiss each other!

Und weil sie sich nicht mehr zu fürchten brauchten, so gingen sie in das Haus der Hexe hinein. Da standen in allen Ecken Kasten mit Perlen und Edelsteinen. "Die sind noch besser als Kieselsteine," sagte Hänsel und steckte in seine Taschen, was hinein wollte. Und Gretel sagte:

"Ich will auch etwas mit nach Haus bringen," und füllte sein Schürzchen voll. "Aber jetzt wollen wir fort," sagte Hänsel, "damit wir aus dem Hexenwald herauskommen."

Als sie aber ein paar Stunden gegangen waren, gelangten sie an ein großes Wasser. "Wir können nicht hinüber," sprach Hänsel, "ich seh keinen Steg und keine Brücke." - "Hier fährt auch kein Schlffchen," antwortete Gretel, "aber da schwimmt eine weiße Ente, wenn ich sie bitte, so hilft sie uns hinüber."
Da rief sie: "Entchen, Entchen, Da steht Gretel und Hänsel. Kein Steg und keine Brücke, Nimm uns auf deinen weißen Rücken."

Das Entchen kam auch heran, und Hänsel setzte sich auf und bat sein Schwesterchen, sich zu ihm zu setzen. "Nein," antwortete Gretel, "es wird dem Entchen zu schwer, es soll uns nacheinander hinüberbringen."
Das tat das gute Tierchen, und als sie glücklich drüben waren und ein Weilchen fortgingen, da kam ihnen der Wald immer bekannter und immer bekannter vor, und endlich erblickten sie von weitem ihres Vaters Haus.
Da fingen sie an zu laufen, stürzten in die Stube hinein und fielen ihrem Vater um den Hals. Der Mann hatte keine frohe Stunde gehabt, seitdem er die Kinder im Walde gelassen hatte, die Frau aber war gestorben.

And as they had no longer any need to fear her, they went into the witch's house, and in every corner there stood chests full of pearls and jewels. 'These are far better than pebbles!' said Hansel, and thrust into his pockets whatever could be got in, and Gretel said:

'I, too, will take something home with me,' and filled her pinafore full. 'But now we must be off,' said Hansel, 'that we may get out of the witch's forest.'

When they had walked for two hours, they came to a great stretch of water. 'We cannot cross,' said Hansel, 'I see no foot-plank, and no bridge.' 'And there is also no ferry,' answered Gretel, 'but a white duck is swimming there: if I ask her, she will help us over.'

Then she cried: 'Little duck, little duck, dost thou see, Hansel and Gretel are waiting for thee? There's never a plank, or bridge in sight, Take us across on thy back so white.'

The duck came to them, and Hansel seated himself on its back, and told his sister to sit by him. 'No,' replied Gretel, 'that will be too heavy for the little duck; she shall take us across, one after the other.'
The good little duck did so, and when they were once safely across and had walked for a short time, the forest seemed to be more and more familiar to them, and at length they saw from afar their father's house.
Then they began to run, rushed into the parlour, and threw themselves round their father's neck. The man had not known one happy hour since he had left the children in the forest; the woman, however, was dead.

Gretel schüttelte sein Schürzchen aus, daß die Perlen und Edelsteine in der Stube herumsprangen, und Hänsel warf eine Handvoll nach der andern aus seiner Tasche dazu.

Da hatten alle Sorgen ein Ende, und sie lebten in lauter Freude zusammen.

Mein Märchen ist aus, dort lauft eine Maus, wer sie fängt, darf sich eine große Pelzkappe daraus machen.

Gretel emptied her pinafore until pearls and precious stones ran about the room, and Hansel threw one handful after another out of his pocket to add to them.

Then all anxiety was at an end, and they lived together in perfect happiness.

My tale is done, there runs a mouse; whosoever catches it, may make himself a big fur cap out of it.

THE WHITE ROSE

The **White Rose** (die **Weiße Rose**) was a non-violent, intellectual resistance group in Nazi Germany led by students from the University of Munich. The group conducted an anonymous leaflet and graffiti campaign that called for active opposition to the Nazi regime.

Their activities started in Munich 27 June 1942. The activities ended with the arrest of the core group by the Gestapo 18 February 1943. Hans and Sophie Scholl were handing out flyers at the Ludwig Maximilian University of Munich when they were caught by the custodian, Jakob Schmid, who informed the Gestapo. They, as well as other members and supporters of the group who carried on distributing the pamphlets, faced show trials by the Nazi People's Court (*Volksgerichtshof*), and many of them were sentenced to death or imprisonment.

Hans and Sophie Scholl and Christoph Probst were executed by guillotine four days after their arrest. During the trial, Sophie interrupted the judge multiple times. No defendants were given any opportunity to speak.

The group wrote, printed, and initially distributed their pamphlets in the greater Munich region. Later, secret carriers brought copies to other cities, mostly in the southern parts of Germany. In total, the White Rose authored six leaflets, which were multiplied and spread, about 15,000 copies. In their second leaflet, they denounced the persecution and mass murder of the Jews.

22 February 1943 they were sentenced to death by the People's Court, led by Judge-President Roland Freisler. They were executed by guillotine the same day in the Stadelheim Prison. Their grave is in the adjacent Perlacher Forst cemetery (grave number 73-1-18/19).

JUNE 17, 1953

The East German uprising of 1953 occurred from 16 to 17 June. It began with a strike by construction workers in East Berlin against work quotas during the Sovietization process in East Germany.

Demonstrations in East Berlin turned into a widespread uprising against the government of East Germany and the Socialist Unity Party, involving an estimated one million people in about 700 localities. The protests against declining living standards and Sovietization policies led to a wave of strikes and protests that threatened to overthrow the East German government.

The uprising in East Berlin was violently suppressed by tanks of the Soviet forces in Germany, while demonstrations continued in more than 500 towns and villages for several more days before dying out.

In 1953, West Berlin renamed part of the Charlottenburger Chaussee *Straße des 17. Juni* to commemorate the uprising.

The uprising is commemorated in *"Die Lösung"*, a poem by Bertolt Brecht.

Judge Bill Swann

Die Lösung	**The Solution**
Nach dem Aufstand des 17. Juni	After the uprising of the 17th of June
Ließ der Sekretär des Schriftstellerverbands	The Secretary of the Writers' Union
In der Stalinallee Flugblätter verteilen	Had leaflets distributed on the Stalinallee
Auf denen zu lesen war, daß das Volk	Stating that the people
Das Vertrauen der Regierung verscherzt habe	Had forfeited the confidence of the government
	And could only win it back
Und es nur durch verdoppelte Arbeit zurückerobern könne. Wäre es da	By increased work quotas. Would it not in that case be simpler
Nicht doch einfacher, die Regierung	for the government
Löste das Volk auf und	To dissolve the people
Wählte ein anderes?	And elect another?

JIM PARROT'S 1974
CHATTANOOGA DECISION

In 1974 and 1975 I clerked for Judge Jim Parrott on the Tennessee Court of Appeals. Judge Parrott's seven-page opinion was a painful decision. It made everyone in Chattanooga mad. My boss took a lot of heat. It was a necessary decision--as you will agree when you read it. I am proud of this decision, proud of my boss, and proud of me, because I wrote the opinion.

IN THE COURT OF APPEALS OF TENNESSEE
EASTERN SECTION

DECEMBER 12, 1974
JOHN A. PARKER, Clerk

STATE OF TENNESSEE, EX REL) FROM THE CIRCUIT COURT FOR HAMILTON COUNTY HON. DAVID TOM WALKER, JUDGE

-vs-

ROBERT STRICKLAND and
DEWAYNE STRICKLAND

EDWARD E. DAVIS and ROBERT BATSON OF CHATTANOOGA
FOR STATE OF TENNESSEE

JESSE O. FARR OF CHATTANOOGA FOR
ROBERT AND DEWAYNE STRICKLAND

OPINION

Parrott, J.

In this appeal we are concerned with whether two juveniles shall stand trial as adults. Both the Juvenile and Circuit Courts of Hamilton County answered in the affirmative. We are unable to reach that result.

On February 12, 1973, Robert and DeWayne Strickland, fifteen and sixteen years of age, came under suspicion of an armed robbery and rape which had taken place the preceding evening. A number of detectives went to the Strickland home on the evening of February 12, picked up Robert and DeWayne, and took them to police headquarters for questioning. The youths denied any involvement in the incident. After inconclusive questioning, the boys were photographed, fingerprinted and released. This first session with the police lasted approximately from 11:00 p. m. to 3:00 a. m.

After further investigation, which included circulation of the youths' photographs, the police determined that more questioning was in order. On the afternoon of February 19, the police had DeWayne's high school coach bring him to headquarters; in response to a telephone call, Robert's parents brought him. This second session lasted--there is some disagreement in the record--around fourteen hours.

On both occasions, the Strickland boys were interrogated separately. At times the interrogation was intense, heated, loud and coercive in atmosphere. Although one or both of the Strickland parents were at the police headquarters the entire time, each boy underwent some questioning apart from a parent. The interrogations culminated the second night in each boy's indicating that he waived his constitutional rights.

"Their father," the brief for the State relates, "told them to tell the truth, and after their rights were read to them slowly, they never refused to speak and never asked for an attorney. At 10:45 p.m. on February 19, 1973, DeWayne waived his constitutional rights after they were repeatedly explained to him one at a time, and recounted his actions on the night of the crime.

. . . In a similar manner, at 12:55 a.m. on February 20, 1973, after four other juveniles including his brother had confessed, Robert Strickland waived his constitutional rights after going over them individually and also confessed his participation in the crime."

Only after these two sessions, held a week apart, had resulted successfully for the State, if we may use that phrase, were the two boys placed under the jurisdiction of the juvenile court.

A hearing was conducted in March in the Juvenile Court for Hamilton County which resulted in both boys being transferred to the Criminal Court of Hamilton County to stand trial as adults. (On May 11, 1973, a victim of the rape and armed robbery died; the charge of murder was added to the State's case.) An appeal of the transfer to criminal court was taken to the Circuit Court of Hamilton County, where a de novo review was held as to whether the statutory requirements for transfer from juvenile court had been met. The circuit court determined those requirements had been met, and the defendants have perfected this appeal.

The statutory requirements for transfer of a case from juvenile court are quite clear. T.C.A. 37-234 requires that after a petition has been filed alleging delinquency, the court may, before hearing the petition on its merits, transfer a child to the sheriff of the county to be dealt with as an adult in the appropriate court. The child will be treated as an adult if four conditions are met. The statutory requirements are:

(1) the child was sixteen (16) or more years of age at the time of the alleged conduct; or the child was fifteen (15) or more years of age at the time of the alleged conduct if the offense charged included murder, rape, robbery with a deadly weapon or kidnapping;

(2) a hearing on whether the transfer should be made is held in conformity with §§37-224, 37-226 and 37-227;

(3) notice in writing of the time, place, and purpose of the hearing is given to the child and his parents, guardian, or other custodian at least three (3) days before the hearing;

(4) the court finds that there are reasonable grounds to believe that
(i) the child committed the delinquent act alleged;
(ii) the child is not amenable to treatment or rehabilitation as a juvenile through available facilities;
(iii) the child is not committable to an institution for the mentally retarded or mentally ill; and
(iv) the interests of the community require that the child be placed under legal restraint or discipline.

In this case it appears condition (1) was met in fact. Condition (3) was met in substance via actual notice. Condition (4) may or may not have been met. We would, however, like to register our dismay as to the State's cursory presentation of proof as to subhead (ii) of condition (4); i.e., amenability and existing facilities. The sufficiency of their case on both points is open to question. The record would seem to suggest that the State felt a trial as adults of these particular defendants could be obtained with only nominal attention to the statutory safeguards of condition (4).

The record, in its silence, discloses that condition (2) has not been met.

T.C.A. 37-234(a)(2) states that the juvenile hearing, on whether a transfer should be made to another court for the purpose of standing trial as an adult, must be held in conformity with T.C.A. 37-224, 37-226 and 37-227. Section 37-227 reads in pertinent part:

37-227. Basic Rights–Confessions–Sufficiency.–

(a) A party is entitled to the opportunity to introduce evidence and otherwise be heard in his own behalf and to cross-examine adverse witnesses.

(b) A child charged with a delinquent act need not be a witness against or otherwise incriminate himself. <u>An extra judicial statement, if obtained in the course of violation of this chapter or which would be constitutionally inadmissible in a criminal proceeding, shall not be used against him</u> . . . (emphasis supplied.)

It is apparent that the admissibility of the confession in this case raises serious constitutional questions. It is possible, for example, that the confessions were in no sense voluntary, but were exacted in an atmosphere of coercion from physically and emotionally spent suspects. There is the further question that these particular defendants may not have knowingly and intelligently waived their rights to counsel and silence, given their ages and decidedly subnormal mental development. Both are classed in the "borderline defective" range of mental capability.

Unfortunately, the State's inability to follow the prescriptions of the statutes does not require us to address ourselves to the questions of constitutional admissibility of the confessions obtained because those extra-judicial statements were "obtained in the course of violation of this [juvenile] chapter."

It will be seen that Sec. 37-227(b) is expansive in its protection of juveniles. Not only are they entitled to the constitutional rights of adults accorded juveniles of every state, In re Gault, 387 U.S. 1, 87 S.Ct. 1428, 18 L.Ed. 2d 527 (1967), they are also allowed to exclude any of their statements obtained in the course of violation of juvenile chapter of Tennessee. That means plainly and simply that the chapter must be tracked or the statements will be inadmissible.

It is clear from the record in this case that the requirements of the juvenile statute have not been adhered to. T.C.A. 37-215(a) states:

37-215. Custody–Release to proper party–Warrant for custody.

(a) A person taking a child into custody, shall directly with all reasonable speed:

(1) release the child to his parents, guardian or other custodian upon their promise to bring the child before the court when requested by the court, unless his detention or shelter care is warranted or required under §37-214; or

(2) bring the child before the court or deliver him to a detention or shelter care facility designated by the court or to a medical facility if the child is believed to suffer from a serious physical condition or illness which requires prompt treatment. He shall promptly give notice thereof, together with a reason for taking the child into custody, to a parent, guardian, or other custodian and to the court. Any temporary detention or questioning of the child necessary to comply

with this subsection shall conform to the procedures and conditions prescribed in this chapter and rules of court.

The Strickland boys were twice taken into custody for the purpose of questioning. Those custodies were lengthy. They were not brought before the juvenile court "directly with all reasonable speed." T.C.A. 37-215(a)(2). They were not in any sense "released" to their parents, T.C.A. 37-215(a)(2), by Mr. Strickland's following the boys to headquarters. And they were not the less in custody by virtue of their parents' presence at headquarters.

We believe the statute means what it says and the courts should not uphold efforts to circumvent its dictates. In clear language the statute requires that a child taken into custody shall be brought before the court in one of two ways: either by taking him there directly, or by having the parents bring him there when requested. Temporary detention or questioning is expressis verbis brought under the requirement.

It might be urged that T.C.A. 37-215(a)(1) provides for police interrogation by means of its reference to T.C.A. 37-214, which provides for detention or care required to protect the person or property of others, or because the child may abscond from the jurisdiction of the court. However, this argument fails due to T.C.A. 37-216, which designates approved places of detention and does not include detention in a police station:

37-216. Place of detention.–

(a) A child alleged to be delinquent or unruly may be detained only in:

(1) a licensed foster home or a home approved by the court;

(2) a facility operated by a licensed child welfare agency;

(3) a detention home or center for delinquent children which is under the direction or supervision of the court or other public authority or of a private agency approved by the court; or

(4) any other suitable place or facility designated or operated by the court. The child may be detained in a jail or other facility for the detention of adults only if other facilities in paragraph (3) above are not available, the detention is in a room separate and removed from those for adults, it appears to the satisfaction of the court that public safety and protection reasonably require detention, and it so orders.

We hold that a hearing on the transfer of the Strickland boys to Hamilton County Criminal Court was not held in conformity with T.C.A. 37-227, as is required by T.C.A. 37-234.

Further, it must be noted that without the extra-judicial statements of the juveniles, which we have held to be inadmissible because they were obtained in violation of the juvenile chapter, there remains no evidence to support the circuit judge's findings that the defendants may be tried as adults. Thus, the circuit judge's findings and order cannot be permitted to stand.

It results the cause is remanded to the circuit court for proceedings not inconsistent with this opinion. For the reasons hereinabove given, the confessions shall not be used as evidence in any proceeding held under Title 37-101 et seq.

James W. Parrott, Judge

CONCUR:
Clifford E. Sanders, J.
Houston M. Goddard, J.

There was an earlier painful opinion in Chattanooga. It was in 1906. Once again an opinion made everyone mad in Chattanooga. The opinion was written by Justice Holmes, but the critical grant of *habeas corpus* in the case was done by Justice Harlan. He was the one who took the heat, the one who was vilified by Chattanoogans.

United States v. Shipp, 203 U.S. 563, dealt with a lynching.

Ed Johnson, a black man, had been convicted in Hamilton County of the rape of a white woman, Nevada Taylor, at the trolley station at the base of Lookout Mountain. He was sentenced to death. 3 March 1906, Johnson's black lawyer, Noah Walter Parden, filed a writ of *habeas corpus*. He alleged that Johnson's constitutional rights had been violated. Specifically, Parden argued that all blacks had been systematically excluded from both the grand jury considering the original indictment of Johnson and the trial jury considering Johnson's case.

Parden further argued that Ed Johnson had been substantively denied the right to counsel, because he, Parden, had been too intimidated by the threats of mob violence to file motions for a change of venue, a continuance, or a new trial. Parden argued Johnson had been deprived of due process and because of that was about to lose his life. And lose his life he did.

Parden was not the only hero in this sad story. Presbyterian minister T. Hooke McCallie, one of the first ministers of First Presbyterian Church on what is now McCallie Avenue, preached for peace from the pulpit and on the street. He later was one of the founders of the McCallie school on the McCallie family farm on Missionary Ridge. The McCallie family were all devout Presbyterians.

10 March 1906 Johnson's petition for *habeas corpus* was initially denied, and he was remanded to the custody of Hamilton County Sheriff Joseph F. Shipp, with the stipulation

that Johnson have 10 days to file further appeals. His appeal to the Supreme Court was granted by Justice Harlan on March 17 and subsequently by the entire court on March 19.

However, even though advised of Harlan's *habeas corpus* ruling by telegram on 17 March–and the case and ruling being given full coverage by Chattanooga's evening newspapers that day--the case against Shipp and his chief jailer said that they had nonetheless allowed a mob to enter the Hamilton County Jail and lynch Johnson on the city's Walnut Street Bridge. The mob riddled him with bullets and pinned a note to his body: "To Justice Harlan. Come and get your nigger now."

The Supreme Court decided that the action constituted contempt of court because Sheriff Shipp, with full knowledge of the court's ruling, chose to ignore his duties to protect a prisoner.

Sheriff Shipp and several others were convicted of contempt of court. Shipp and two of his colleagues were sentenced to 90 days imprisonment, and three others were sentenced to 60 days imprisonment. In the court's words, "Shipp not only made the work of the mob easy, but in effect aided and abetted it."

However, when Shipp was released he continued to swear that he was innocent. He was welcomed back like a hero.

Threatened with violence, Noah Walter Parden had to leave the state, never to return.

February 2000, ninety-four years after the lynching, Hamilton County Criminal Judge Doug Meyer overturned Johnson's conviction, ruling that Johnson did not receive a fair trial because of the all-white jury and the judge's refusal to move the trial from Chattanooga.

NEWT GINGRICH, DEC. 21, 2020, ON BIDEN'S ELECTION

A smart friend of mine who is a moderate liberal asked why I was not recognizing Joe Biden's victory. The friend made the case that Mr. Biden had gotten more votes, and historically we recognize the person with the most votes. Normally, we accept the outcome of elections just as we accept the outcomes of sporting events. So, my friend asked why was 2020 different?

Having spent more than four years watching the left "resist" President Donald Trump and focus entirely on undoing and undermining the 2016 election, it took me several days to understand the depth of my own feelings.

As I thought about it, I realized my anger and fear were not narrowly focused on votes. My unwillingness to relax and accept that the election grew out of a level of outrage and alienation unlike anything I had experienced in more than 60 years of involvement in public affairs.

The challenge is that I, and other conservatives, are not disagreeing with the left within a commonly understood world. We live in alternative worlds. The left's world is mostly the established world of the forces who have been dominant for most of my life.

My world is the populist rebellion which believes we are being destroyed, our liberties are being cancelled, and our religions are under assault. Note the new Human Rights Campaign to decertify any religious school which does not accept secular sexual values, and that many Democrat governors have kept casinos open while closing churches though the COVID-19 pandemic.

In 2016, I supported an outsider candidate, who was rough around the edges and in the Andrew Jackson school of controversial assaults on the old order. When my candidate won, it was blamed on the Russians. We now know, four years later, that Hillary Clinton's own team financed the total lie that fueled this attack.

Members of the FBI twice engaged in criminal acts to help it along — once in avoiding prosecution of someone who had deleted 33,000 emails and had a subordinate use a hammer to physically destroy hard drives, and a second time by lying to FISA judges to destroy Gen. Michael Flynn and spy on then-candidate Donald Trump and his team.

The national liberal media aided and abetted every step of the way. All this was purely an attempt to cripple the new president and lead to the appointment of a special counsel, who ultimately produced nothing.

Now, people in my world are told it is time to stop resisting and cooperate with the new president. But we remember that the Democrats wanted to cooperate with Mr. Trump so much that they began talking about his impeachment before he even took office. The *Washington Post* ran a story on Democrat impeachment plots the day of the inauguration.

In fact, nearly 70 Democratic lawmakers boycotted his inauguration. A massive left-wing demonstration was staged in Washington the day after, where Madonna announced she dreamed of blowing up the White House, to widespread applause.

These same forces want me to cooperate with their new president. I find myself adopting the Nancy Pelosi model of constant resistance. Nothing I have seen from Mr. Biden since the election offers me any hope that he will reach out to the more than 74 million Americans who voted for President Trump.

So, I am not reacting to the votes so much as to the whole election environment. When Twitter and Facebook censored the oldest and fourth largest newspaper (founded by Alexander Hamilton) because it accurately reported news that could hurt Mr. Biden's chances, where were the *New York Times* and *Washington Post*? The truth of the Hunter Biden story is now becoming impossible to avoid or conceal.

The family of the Democrat nominee for president received at least $5 million from an entity controlled by our greatest adversary. It was a blatant payoff, and most Americans who voted for Mr. Biden never heard of it, or were told before the election it was Russian disinformation. Once they did hear of it, 17% said they would have switched their votes, according to a poll by the Media Research Center. That's the entire election. The censorship worked exactly as intended.

Typically, newspapers and media outlets band together when press freedom is threatened by censorship. Where was the sanctimonious "democracy dies in darkness?" Tragically, the *Washington Post* is now part of the darkness.

But this is just a start. When Twitter censors four of five Rush Limbaugh tweets in one day, I fear for the country. When these monolithic Internet giants censor the president of the United States, I fear for the country. When I see elite billionaires like Mark Zuckerburg spend $400 million to hire city governments to maximize turnout in specifically Democratic districts without any regard to election spending laws or good governance standards, I fear for the country. When I read that Apple has a firm rule of never irritating China, and I watch the NBA kowtow to Beijing, I fear for our country.

When I watch story after story about election fraud being spiked, without even the appearance of journalistic due diligence or curiosity, I know something is sick.

The election process itself was the final straw in creating the crisis of confidence which is accelerating and deepening for many millions of Americans. Aside from a constant stream of allegations of outright fraud, there are some specific outrages, any one of which was likely enough to swing the entire election.

Officials in virtually every swing state broke their states' own laws to send out millions of ballots or ballot applications to every registered voter. It was all clearly documented in the Texas lawsuit, which was declined by the U.S. Supreme Court based on Texas' procedural standing, not the merits of the case. That's the election.

In addition, it's clear that virtually every swing state essentially suspended normal requirements for verifying absentee ballots. Rejection rates were an order of magnitude lower than in a normal year. In Georgia, rejection rates dropped from 6.5% in 2016 to 0.2% in 2020. In Pennsylvania, it went from 1% in 2016 to .003% in 2020. Nevada fell from 1.6% to .75%. There is no plausible explanation other than that they were counting a huge number of ballots, disproportionately for Mr. Biden, that normally would not have passed muster. That's the election.

The entire elite liberal media lied about the timeline of the COVID-19 vaccine. They blamed President Trump for the global pandemic even as he did literally everything top scientists instructed. In multiple debates, the moderators outright stated that he was lying about the U.S. having a vaccine before the end of the year.

The unanimously never-Trump debate commission spiked the second debate at a critical time in order to hurt President Trump. If there had been one more debate like the final one, it likely would have been pivotal.

But any one of those things alone is enough for Trump supporters to think we have been robbed by a ruthless establishment, which is likely to only get more corrupt and aggressive if it gets away with these blatant acts. For more than four years, the entire establishment mobilized against the elected president of the United States as though they were an immune system trying to kill a virus. Now, they are telling us we are undermining democracy.

You have more than 74 million voters who supported President Trump despite everything, and given the election mess the number could easily be significantly higher. The truth is tens of millions of Americans are deeply alienated and angry. If Mr. Biden governs from the left, and he will almost certainly be forced to, that number will grow rapidly.

Given this environment, I have no interest in legitimizing the father of a son who Chinese Communist Party members boast about buying. Nor do I have any interest in pretending that the current result is legitimate or honorable. It is simply the final stroke of a four-year establishment-media power grab. It has been perpetrated by people who have broken the law, cheated the country of information, and smeared those of us who believe in America over China, history over revisionism, and the liberal ideal of free expression over cancel culture.

I write this in genuine sorrow, because I think we are headed toward a serious, bitter struggle in America. This extraordinary, coordinated four-year power grab threatens the fabric of our country and the freedom of every American.

LEE CHILD ON
JACK REACHER

This is a long and excellent essay about writing effectively. It is also about how to earn a living as a writer. I have made alterations and omissions in the flow here and there. I hope you enjoy it. It's down-to-earth, simple, and straightforward. It is written in the first person, with Lee Child speaking.
–Judge Bill Swann

Jack Reacher made his first appearance in print 17 March 1997 when Putnam published *Killing Floor* in the United States. This was Reacher's debut, and mine also. But I can trace his genesis backward at least to New Year's Eve 1988.

Back then I worked for a commercial television station in Manchester, England. I was eleven years into a career as a presentation director, which is a little like an air traffic controller for the airwaves. In February 1988, the UK commercial network had started twenty-four-hour broadcasting. For a year before that, management had been talking about how to staff the new expanded commitment. None of us really wanted to work nights. Management didn't really want to hire extra people. Impasse. What broke it was the offer of a huge raise.

135

We took it, and by New Year's Eve we were ten fat and happy months into the new contract. I went to a party, but didn't feel much like celebrating. Not that I wasn't content in the short term: I sleep better by day than night, and I like being up and about when the world is quiet and lonely, and for sure I was having a ball with the new salary. But I knew in my bones that management resented the raise, and I knew that the new contract was in fact the beginning of the end.

Sooner or later, we would all be fired in revenge. I felt it was only a matter of time. Nobody agreed with me except one woman. At the party, in a quiet moment, she asked me, "What are you going to do when this is all over?" I said, "I'm going to write books." Why that answer? And why then?

I had always been an insatiable reader. All genres, all the time, but very unstructured. I naturally gravitated toward crime, adventure, and thrillers, but for a long time in the UK we lacked genre stores and fan magazines, and of course the Internet hadn't started yet, so there was no effective network capable of leading a reader from one thing to the next. As a result, I had come across some very obscure stuff, while being completely ignorant of many major figures.

In February 1988 while the ink was still drying on our new TV contracts I took a vacation in the Yucatán. I flew back via Miami, and picked up John D. MacDonald's *The Lonely Silver Rain* at a bookstall in the airport. I had never heard of MacDonald or Travis McGee. I read the book on the plane back to London and loved it. I thought, "I wonder if it's part of a series?" Hah! I was back in the States at Easter that year and bought every McGee title I could find, which added up to about a linear yard's worth.

Nobody needs me to sing MacDonald's praises, but that yard of books did more for me than provide excellent entertainment. For some reason the McGee books spoke to me like textbooks. I felt I could see what MacDonald was doing, and why, and how, as if I could see the skeleton beneath the skin. I read them all that summer, and by New Year's Eve I was completely sure that when the ax fell, I wanted to do what MacDonald had done.

I could stay in the entertainment business, but work for myself in the world of books. It took six years for the ax to fall. But fall it did, and so it came time to make good on that earlier ambition. I went to W.H. Smith's store in the Manchester Arndale mall–which the IRA destroyed a year later–and bought three legal pads, a pencil, a pencil sharpener, and an eraser. The bill was a penny under four pounds, which was about six bucks at the time.

Then I sat down with my purchases and let years of half-formed thoughts take shape. But not just six years of thoughts–now I have to take the process back another thirty years or so, to the point when my reading habit first took hold.

I had found that I liked some things, and disliked other things. I had always been drawn to outlaws. I liked cleverness and ingenuity. I liked the promise of intriguing revelations. I disliked a hero who was generally smart but did something stupid three-quarters of the way through the book, merely to set up the last part of the action. Detectives on the trail who walked into rooms and got hit over the head from behind just didn't do it for me.

And I liked winners. I was vaguely uneasy with the normal story arc that has a guy lose, lose, lose before he wins in the end. I liked to see something done spectacularly well. In sports, I liked crushing victories rather than ninth-inning nail-biters.

Some of my reading was directed, of course, in school. I was part of probably the last generation ever to receive a classical English education. I read Latin and Greek and Old English, all the ancient myths and medieval sagas and poems. I met the "knight errant" at the source.

137

Then I took a law degree at university. I never intended to be a lawyer, but the subject knit together all my nonfiction interests--history, politics, economics, sociology, and language. Legal language strives for concision and avoids ambiguity. The result is inevitably dull, but all that striving and avoiding really teaches a person how to write.

Then I went to work in the theater, and developed a phobia. Back then there was plenty of experimental theater, some of it good, most of it awful. The worst of it was run by people who saw their minimal audiences as badges of honor. "The public is too stupid to understand us," they would say.

I hated that attitude. To me, entertainment was a transaction. You do it, they watch it, then it exists. Like a Zen question: If you put on a show, and nobody comes, have you in fact put on a show at all? So for me, the audience mattered from the start. Which helped me thrive in television. And along the way I discovered I was the audience. We were generally doing quality mass-market entertainment, but even so, some guys were conscious of slumming. Not me. G. K. Chesterton once said of Charles Dickens, "Dickens didn't write what people wanted. Dickens wanted what people wanted." I would never compare myself to Charles Dickens, but I know exactly what Chesterton meant.

So, at thirty-nine years of age, after maybe thirty-five years of conscious experience, I sat down and opened the first of my three legal pads on my dining room table and lined up my pencil and sharpener and eraser and ... thought some more. I came up with three specific conclusions.

First: Character is king. There are probably fewer than six books every century remembered specifically for their plots. People remember characters. Same with television. Who remembers the Lone Ranger? Everybody. Who remembers any actual Lone Ranger story lines? Nobody. So, my lead character had to carry the whole weight . . . and there was a lot of weight to carry. Remember, I was broke and out of work.

Second conclusion: If you can see a bandwagon, it's too late to get on. I think the person who said that to me was talking about investment issues—as if I had anything to invest—but it seemed an excellent motto for entertainment, as well. It's a crowded field. Why do what everyone else is doing? So, I was going to have to do something a little different. The series that were then well under way—and most that were just starting out—were, it seemed to me, when carefully analyzed, soap operas. (Which, to me, is not a derogatory term. Soap opera is an incredibly powerful narrative engine, and soap operas had put food on my table for eighteen years. Lots of it, and high quality.)

Lead characters were *primi inter pares* in a repertory cast, locations were fixed and significant, employment was fixed and significant. In other words, series heroes had partners, friends, jobs, apartments, favorite bars, favorite restaurants, neighbors, family, even dogs and cats. They jogged, worked out, and had pastimes. They had bills to pay and issues to resolve. If you can see a bandwagon, it's too late to get on. I was going to have to avoid all that stuff.

But, the third conclusion, and the most confounding conclusion: You can't design a character too specifically. I knew in my bones that to think too carefully would produce a laundry list of imagined qualities and virtues and would result in a flat, boring, cardboard character. I would be consulting a mental checklist: "I need to satisfy this demographic . . . check . . . and please these people . . . check . ." until I had a guy with all the spark and life beaten out of him. So I quite self-consciously pushed that thirty-five-year soup of ideas and influences into the distant background and decided to relax and see what would come along.

Jack Reacher came along. I was interested in dislocation and alienation, and I had noticed that people who have spent their lives in the military have trouble adjusting to civilian life afterward. It's like moving to a different planet. So I wrote a character who had been first a military brat, then a military officer, and was now plunged unwillingly into the civilian world. And because the books would be broadly crime novels, I made him an ex–military cop in order to give him plausible familiarity with investigative procedures and forensics and so on.

Those twin decisions gave him a double layer of alienation. First, his transition from the rough, tough world of the army made him a fish out of water in civilian life, which situation was then further reinforced by any law enforcement officer's separation from the rest of the population. It's easier to be rootless and alienated in a giant country like America. Alienation in a tiny, crowded island like Britain is of a different order, almost wholly psychological rather than physical or literal. I like reading the internal, claustrophobic British books, but I didn't want to write them. I wanted big, rangy plots; big landscapes; big skies.

Jack Reacher's status as a former officer happened instinctively. Looking back, I clearly wanted to tap into the medieval knight-errant paradigm, and a knight-errant has to have been a knight in the first place. I thought a West Point history and a rank of major would be suitable. In literary terms it was an important choice, but later I realized it has plausibility issues. His whole personality, approach, and implied past experiences make it much more likely that in the real world he would have been a warrant officer, not a commissioned officer.

But to me it was crucial that he should have a certain nobility—which is a strange thing to say about a guy who goes around busting heads as frequently and thoroughly as

Jack Reacher does--but it is clear from subsequent reaction that his "white hat" status depends heavily on our images of and assumptions about rank.

His "white hat" status has tempted readers to classify the series as a set of modern-day Westerns, which is convincing in terms of feel and structure. Some of the novels are just like *Shane,* or a Zane Grey story, or a Lone Ranger episode—lonely, embattled community has a problem; mysterious stranger rides in off the range, solves the problem, rides off into the sunset.

At first he wasn't called Jack Reacher. In fact, he wasn't called anything at all. The part of writing that I find most difficult is coming up with character names. My books are heavily populated with stationery brands and other authors, because when I need to name someone I tend to look around my office helplessly until my eye alights on the front of a notebook or the spine of a book on my shelves. Once or twice I stared out my window until a neighbor walked past, or thought back to the name badge of the last clerk I saw in a store . . . all kinds of people get their names in my books, most of them unwittingly. But obviously the main character's name is important to get right. With luck it will appear in many books, and even be talked about in other contexts.

I started writing with no clear idea of the name. The first book was written in the first person, which meant he didn't need a name until someone else asked what it was, which didn't happen for thirty or so manuscript pages. Then a police detective asked, "Name?"

I put my pencil down and thought. The best I could come up with was Franklin, as I recall. But I wasn't happy with it. Then I went shopping. Part of the problem with not currently having a day job was, well, I didn't have a day job, and my wife therefore assumed that after many years of solo struggle she now had help with chores. So she asked me to go to the supermarket with her, to carry stuff home. I'm a big guy; she's a small woman. She was also a worried woman, although she was hiding it well. Our life savings were disappearing, and regular paychecks were merely distant memories.

In the supermarket—and this is a common experience for tall men—a little old lady approached me and said, "You're a nice tall gentleman, so would you reach that can for me?" My wife said to me, "If this writing thing doesn't work out, you can always be a reacher in a supermarket." I thought, great name!

And I used it, and I smile now when I read Internet commentary imagining I specified the name for its forward-going, striving, progressive implications. His first name came from conclusion number two: Don't do what the others are doing. At the time there was a miniature rash of characters with cute or complex first names. So I looked for the simplest and plainest name I could find. I chose Jack, and not as a diminutive for John, either. It's just Jack.

One of my grandfathers was called Harry, which most people assumed was a diminutive for Henry, but it wasn't. Harry was on his birth certificate. In my third book, *Tripwire*, there's a passage that starts: "Reacher had been named Jack by his father, who was a plain New Hampshire Yankee with an implacable horror of anything fancy."

I wanted to underpin Reacher's blunt and straightforward manner with a blunt and straightforward name. I didn't think the character would have worked with, say, MacNaughten Lawrence for a name. Still don't. Even though the first name could have been abbreviated to "Mac" on nearly all occasions, the hidden truth on his official papers would have implied something that I didn't want implied. So, he's an ex–military officer, he's American, he's alienated, he struggles to participate effectively in civilian society, and he has a plain name.

And he's huge. He's six feet five inches tall, and around two hundred and fifty pounds, all of it muscle. In *Tripwire*, after he's been doing physical labor in the sun for a spell, he's described as looking "like a condom stuffed with walnuts." No one in his right mind would mess with him. I had in mind the kind of intimidating physical presence that pro footballers have (relaxed, utterly sure of themselves) but in Reacher's case with a barely visible hint of danger. (In fact, in *One Shot*, he admits to having played football for Army while at West Point, but that his career was limited to only one game. "Why?" someone asks. "Were you injured?" "No," he replies. "I was too violent.")

His physical presence is another offshoot of conclusion number two: Don't do what the others are doing. And for a long time what the others had been doing was making their protagonists more and more flawed and vulnerable. Way back, it had been a welcome development to move away from the uniformly lantern-jawed he-men that had crowded the genre. Heroes became smaller, realistically afraid, physically unexceptional. On the emotional side, they became battered. They were alcoholics, recovering alcoholics, divorced recovering alcoholics, divorced recovering alcoholics living in cabins in the woods and traumatized by professional mistakes. Literal and metaphorical bullets were lodged near hearts. There was an overwhelming feeling of incipient failure and melancholy. As with all trends, this one was started by inspired pioneers and then overdone by imitators. By the time I started writing I was tired of it.

I wanted to start over with an old-fashioned hero who had no problems, no issues, and no navel-gazing. His physical competence is really an expression of his mental competence, too. He's a fully-functioning person. And I thought it would be interesting to reverse the paradigm in terms of physical vulnerability.

Usually, a book's hero comes up against people he needs to be afraid of. What if, I asked myself, the hero is the toughest SOB in the valley and others need to be afraid of him? In my fourth book, *Running Blind*, an FBI agent called Blake threatens to leak Reacher's name to a violent psychopath called Petrosian. Blake thinks it's an effective motivator—and in real life and most books it would be.

Reacher has plenty of minor problems. He's awkward in civilian society. He gets around his difficulties by assembling a series of eccentricities that border on the weird. If he doesn't know how something works, he just doesn't participate. He doesn't have a cell phone, doesn't understand text messaging, doesn't grasp e-mail. He doesn't do laundry. He buys cheap clothes, and junks them three or four days later, and buys more.

To him, that's a rigorously rational solution to an evident problem. To us, it's almost autistic. The contrast between his narrow and highly developed skills and his general helplessness humanizes him. It gives him dimension. He has enough problems to make him interesting, but crucially, he himself doesn't know he has these problems. He thinks he's fine. He thinks he's normal. Hence interest without the whiny self-awareness of the "bullet lodged near the heart" guys.

What motivates him? He has no need for or interest in employment. He's not a proactive do-gooder. So why does he get involved in things? Well, partly because of *noblesse oblige*, which is a French chivalric concept that means "nobility obligates," which in other words mandates honorable, generous, and responsible behavior because of high rank or birth. Reacher had the rank and has the skills, and he feels a slightly Marxist obligation "from him who has, to him who needs." Again, that attitude predates the twentieth century by a long way. It shows up in nineteenth-century Western heroes and thirteenth-century European heroes, all the way back to the Greeks, and, we can be sure, much farther back into oral traditions where no written records exist.

Added to which, in Reacher's case, is a cantankerousness that provokes him. In *Persuader*, during a flashback to his military days, he is asked why he became an MP when he could have chosen any other branch of the service. He gives a vague answer, along the lines of wanting to look after the little guy. His questioner is skeptical. She says, disbelievingly, "You care about the little guy?" "Not really," Reacher admits. "I don't really care about the little guy. I just hate the big guy. I hate big smug people who think they can get away with things."

That's what motivates him. The world is full of unfairness and injustice. He can't intervene everywhere. He needs to sense a sneering, arrogant, manipulative opponent in the shadows. Then he'll go to work. Partly because he himself is arrogant. In a sense, each book is a contest between Reacher's arrogance and his opponent's. Arrogance is not an attractive attribute, but I don't hide Reacher's because I think the greatest mistake a series writer can make is to get too chummy with his main character.

I aim to like Reacher just a little less than I hope you will. Because basically a book is a simple psychological transaction. "I'm the main character," the main character announces. The reader asks: "Am I going to like you?" There are several possible answers to that question. The worst is: "Yes, you really are, and I'll tell you why!" But Reacher answers: "You might, or you might not, and either way is fine with me." Because, as an author, I believe that kind of insouciant self-confidence forms a more enduring bond. Does it?

COOKING

CORN PONE

Grandfather Swann made this pone in Covington, Georgia. My father and I kept it up in Tennessee. It is thin and crunchy.

  white or yellow corn meal (not self-rising)
  ½ tsp. salt
  cold water
  olive oil
  preheated 375-degree oven
  real butter to serve with the pone when it is done

Rinse and dry the griddle or skillet if it hasn't been used in a while. Scour it with a wad of paper towel, damp with olive oil. Put a small dollop of oil into the skillet and spread it around covering the entire bottom and sides up about half an inch. The batter will be so thin it will not climb the sides. The skillet or griddle needs to be significantly damp with oil. If there is too much, daub it up with a paper towel.

Put the meal into a medium large bowl. Start with four heaping serving spoons. Add the salt. Turn a cold faucet on slightly, and put the bowl under it for a moment. Mix the batter with one hand. Add water in dribs until it is a thick soup. Dump it onto the center of the griddle or skillet. Pat it down, spreading it out gradually to the edges, rotating the griddle or skillet. The batter should be quite soupy. Jerk the griddle or skillet left and right to spread the batter. If it doesn't reach the edges, mix another batch and dump it in the middle of the first one and pat it out. Repeat the jerk motion.

Make sure the oven is at 375 degrees. Bake for 20 minutes; check. It probably won't be done. It may need five more; check again. It may need another five. Cook until there is ample brown at the edges, and maybe at some of the thin spots.

Serve with real butter.

If taken out of the oven when it is just browning, the pone will be soft and chewable. It is better to wait until it is thin and crunchy.

CAST IRON SKILLETS

For daily cleaning, rinse with hot water, using a stiff nylon brush to remove residue. Use mild dish soap for extremely greasy pans. Don't submerge a hot pan in cold water; it can crack. Towel it dry and apply a light coat of oil while the pan is warm.

When you use it as much as Grandma did, even if you clean it daily, you might notice food starting to stick. That means it's time to re-season the pan.

Seasoning is the process of adhering oil to the surface to create a nonstick coating. New pans are factory-seasoned, but if you have an older pan, here's what to do:

1. Line the lower oven rack with aluminum foil and preheat the oven to 350°.
2. Scrub the pan with hot, soapy water and a stiff brush to remove any rust.
3. Towel it dry and apply a thin coat of vegetable oil to the entire pan—the outside and the handle included.
4. Place it on the top oven rack, upside down; bake for one hour.
5. Turn off the oven and leave the pan inside to cool. Now you're ready to cook.

GRITS THE RIGHT WAY

Ingredients:

- *one teaspoon of salt*
- *one quart of water*
- *butter (never margarine)*
- *one cup old fashioned, stone ground, slow cooking grits (never "five minute," or "quick cooking" grits)*
- *grated cheese or sour cream (optional)*
- *black pepper*

Bring the water and salt to a boil. Grits stick, so put some butter into the boiling water before you whisk in the grits. Turn the heat to low, and put a lid on the pot.

Don't touch anything for twenty minutes, then check the consistency. If it's too wet, keep cooking. When it is done, you can whisk in cheese or sour cream. If not that, whisk in some butter.

Pour into a bowl, dot with butter, and serve. Make sure freshly ground black pepper is on the table.

LOBSTER WITH
SCRAMBLED EGGS

Equipment:

    bowl for mixing eggs
    large cast iron skillet with cast iron lid
    409 spray cleaner
    paper towels for clean up

Ingredients:

    2-3 live Maine lobsters, one and a quarter pounds or larger
    12 eggs
    salt and pepper to taste

Directions:

Break eggs into a bowl but do not scramble.
Heat skillet on stove top until very hot.
Have the cast iron lid ready in one hand.
Throw lobsters into the skillet with your other hand, dump
the eggs in fast, and get that lid on.

When the thrashing stops, the dish is ready.
Correct the seasonings.

<u>Preparation time:</u> 8 minutes
<u>Cook time:</u> 4 minutes
<u>Clean up time:</u> half an hour; use paper towels

RELIGION

THE 23D PSALM

The LORD is my shepherd; I shall not want.
He maketh me to lie down in green pastures:
he leadeth me beside the still waters.

He restoreth my soul: he leadeth me in the
paths of righteousness for his name's sake.

Yea, though I walk through the valley of the
shadow of death, I will fear no evil: for thou art
with me; thy rod and thy staff they comfort me.

Thou preparest a table before me in the
presence of mine enemies: thou anointest my
head with oil; my cup runneth over.

Surely goodness and mercy shall follow me all
the days of my life: and I will dwell in the house
of the LORD for ever.

In 2021 I wrote about the shepherd and his flock, a theme in both the old and new testaments. The 23d Psalm is also about the shepherd and his flock. This time it is a flock of one, the speaker of the psalm. The comfortable and familiar language begins,

> *The Lord is my shepherd; I shall not want.*

That very first word announces monotheism. It is <u>the</u> Lord. Only one Lord, not the multiple gods of the Greeks and the Romans, not the multiple gods of the Egyptians or the Incas. One God, <u>the</u> Lord.

What about this monotheistic God? *"The Lord is."* The Lord simply is. We live and breathe and have our being in this one God.

"The Lord is my shepherd," we read. The take-away word here is "my." The Lord ministers to me. Even to me, even to humble me. My Lord is personal. He is taking care of me. He is addressing my needs. He does this by being my shepherd, my caregiver, my protector.

We are so accustomed to the King James 1611 text that the whole psalm can simply flow over us in a rush of beauty. This is good, but there are individual building blocks in this beauty.

This God who is my shepherd,

> *maketh me to lie down in green pastures: he leadeth me beside the still waters.*

This God, my shepherd, gives me peace. He makes me calm. He takes away my worries. He builds me up. He replenishes my innermost being, my soul:

> *He restoreth my soul: he leadeth me in the paths of righteousness for his name's sake.*

He leads me to correct behavior for the glory of God.

The speaker is not to fear. Even as the sheep and the speaker were protected, bedded down, given water to drink, the speaker is now protected even from death:

> *Yea, though I walk through the valley of the shadow of death, I will fear no evil, for thou art with me.*
>
> *Thy rod and thy staff they comfort me.*

His enemies are nothing to him. He defies them with God's help:

> *Thou preparest a table before me in the presence of mine enemies: thou anointest my head with oil; my cup runneth over.*

God has demonstrated his love. He will follow his paths. He is protected, led. He lives and acts for the glory of God's name, walking in the paths of righteousness.

> *Surely goodness and mercy shall follow me all the days of my life: and I will dwell in the house of the LORD forever.*

John chapter 10 gives us Christ's words: "*I am the good shepherd. I know my own, and my own know me, just as the Father knows me and I know the Father; and I lay down my life for the sheep.*"

ETERNAL LIFE

The gospel of John has many references to eternal life, the most famous being John 3:16:

> For God so loved the world, that he gave his only Son, that whoever believes in him should not perish but have eternal life.

John 3:36 states,

> Whoever believes in the Son has eternal life; whoever does not obey the Son shall not see life, but the wrath of God remains on him.

At John 4:14, Jesus tells the Samaritan woman at the well that,

> Everyone who drinks of this water will be thirsty again, but whoever drinks of the water that I will give him will never be thirsty again. The water that I will give him will become in him a spring of water welling up to eternal life.

At John 5:24, Jesus states,

> *whoever hears my word and believes him who sent me has eternal life. He does not come into judgment, but has passed from death to life.*

In John 6:27, Jesus,

> *Do not work for the food that perishes, but for the food that endures to eternal life, which the Son of Man will give to you.*

At John 6:51 we are told,

> *I am the living bread that came down from heaven. If anyone eats of this bread, he will live forever. And the bread that I will give for the life of the world is my flesh.*

At John 6:54 ff we read:

> *Whoever feeds on my flesh and drinks my blood has eternal life, and I will raise him up on the last day. For my flesh is true food, and my blood is true drink. Whoever feeds on my flesh and drinks my blood abides in me, and I in him. As the living Father sent me, and I live because of the Father, so whoever feeds on me, he also will live because of me. This is the bread that came down from heaven, not like the bread the fathers ate, and died. Whoever feeds on this bread will live forever.*

PETER

It is Peter—the repeatedly bumbling Peter who denied Christ three times—it is this man who in the book of Acts rises to lead the nascent church.

This mature Peter defies those who crucified Christ. He says what must be done: repent and be baptized. He knows who his enemies are, and he is ready for them.

Peter earlier was bumbling, impetuous, a magnet for mistakes. And then he became the rock upon which the church is built. What happened? Two things. Two outpourings of the holy spirit: the one vast outpouring at Pentecost, but also an earlier one: After the crucifixion, Christ appears to the disciples (John 20:21):

> *Jesus said to them again, "Peace be with you. As the Father has sent me, even so I am sending you."*

> *And when he had said this, he breathed on them and said to them, "Receive the Holy Spirit. If you forgive the sins of any, they are forgiven them; if you withhold forgiveness from any, it is withheld."*

LOVE

In the sixth book of the Old Testament the Moabite Ruth says to her Israelite mother in law:

> *Where you go I will go, and where you stay I will stay.*
>
> *Your people will be my people and your God my God.*
>
> *Where you die I will die, and there I will be buried.*
>
> *May the Lord deal with me, be it ever so severely, if even death separates you and me.*

In 1958, Felice and Boudleaux Bryant described love this way for the Everly Brothers:

> *Darling you can count on me*
> *'Til the sun dries up the sea*
> *Until then I'll always be*
> *Devoted to you*

I'll be yours through endless time
I'll adore your charms sublime
Guess by now you'll know that I'm
Devoted to you

Goethe treated love this way in 1774:

Es war ein König in Thule,
Gar treu bis an das Grab,
Dem sterbend seine Buhle
einen goldnen Becher gab.
Es ging ihm nichts darüber,
Er leert' ihn jeden Schmaus;
Die Augen gingen ihm über,
So oft er trank daraus.
Und als er kam zu sterben,
Zählt' er seine Städt' im Reich,
Gönnt' alles seinen Erben,
Den Becher nicht zugleich.
Er saß beim Königsmahle,
Die Ritter um ihn her,
Auf hohem Vätersaale,
Dort auf dem Schloß am Meer.
Dort stand der alte Zecher,
Trank letzte Lebensglut,
Und warf den heiligen Becher
Hinunter in die Flut.
Er sah ihn stürzen, trinken
Und sinken tief ins Meer,
die Augen täten ihm sinken,
Trank nie einen Tropfen mehr

There was a king in Thule,
Was faithful till the grave,
To whom his mistress, dying,
A golden goblet gave.
Nought was to him more precious;
He drained it at every bout;
His eyes with tears run over,
As oft as he drank thereout.
When came his time of dying,
The towns in his land he told,
Nought else to his heir denying
Except the goblet of gold.
He sat at the royal banquet
With his knights of high degree,
In the lofty hall of his fathers
In the castle by the sea.
There stood the old carouser,
And drank the last life-glow;
And hurled the hallowed goblet
Into the tide below.
He saw it plunging and filling,
And sinking deep in the sea:
Then fell his eyelids for ever,
And never more drank he!

AFTERWORD

The afterword is the place where the author says something to wrap up the whole ball of wax.

The most important thing to say, of course, is "Thank you!" to you the reader for the time you have given to *More Kirksey.*" I had fun writing the book. I hope you had at least some fun reading it.

You can tell from <u>*Jim Parrot's 1974 Chattanooga decision*</u> that I am proud of him, and that I owe him a lot. So here is the perfect place for me to say, after so many years, "Thank you, Boss."

Printed in the United States
by Baker & Taylor Publisher Services